Global City Review

Fish Out of Water

FALL 1996 · ISSUE NUMBER EIGHT

EDITOR
Linsey Abrams

SR EDITOR
E. M. Broner

MANAGING EDITOR
Rachel DeNys

ISSUE EDITORS
Patricia Chao, Jennifer Coke, AND
Karen de Balbian Verster

CONTRIBUTING EDITORS
*Marin Gazzaniga, Christina Gombar, Randall Kenan,
Michael Klein, Mary LaChapelle, Susan Thames* AND
Eliot Weinberger

ASSOCIATE EDITORS
*Angie Argabrite, Judy Bloomfield,
Edith Chevat, Lynda Curnyn, Amy Dana,
Diana Estigarribia, Christine Liotta,
Mary McGail, Laurie Piette, Lauren Sanders*
AND *Elizabeth Winston*

PUBLICITY DIRECTOR
Elizabeth England

PUBLISHER
Laurie E. Liss

GLOBAL CITY REVIEW
Fish Out of Water
FALL 1996
NUMBER EIGHT

Global City Review is published twice yearly.
SUBSCRIPTION PRICE: $12 FOR ONE YEAR, $20 FOR TWO YEARS.
INTERNATIONAL: $17 FOR ONE YEAR, $30 FOR TWO YEARS.
INSTITUTIONS: $15 FOR ONE YEAR, $25 FOR TWO YEARS.
MAKE CHECKS PAYABLE TO GLOBAL CITY REVIEW

ALL CORRESPONDENCE SHOULD BE SENT TO:
GLOBAL CITY REVIEW
SIMON H. RIFKIND CENTER FOR THE HUMANITIES
THE CITY COLLEGE OF NEW YORK
138TH AND CONVENT AVENUE
NEW YORK, NY 10031
PLEASE INCLUDE A SASE WITH ALL MANUSCRIPTS.

GLOBAL CITY REVIEW IS DISTRIBUTED BY
CONSORTIUM BOOK SALES & DISTRIBUTION
1-800-283-3572

ISBN: 1-887369-04-X

GLOBAL CITY REVIEW
CONTINUES TO BE PUBLISHED WITH
THE GENEROUS SUPPORT OF
THE SIMON H. RIFKIND CENTER FOR THE HUMANITIES
AT THE CITY COLLEGE OF NEW YORK.
WITH SPECIAL THANKS TO DEAN MARTIN TAMNY.

DESIGN BY CHARLES NIX

LAYOUT AND PRODUCTION BY BRIAN GREENSPAN

Contents

RACE, ETHNICITY, CLASS, GENDER, GENDER PREFERENCE, health status, age—our most basic defining characteristics—can all cause us to feel like outsiders. The voices in *Global City Review's* Fall 1996 issue, *Fish Out of Water,* tell of our sense of displacement in situations that threaten identity, how we adapt and how we don't, and at what price either.

The most literal definition of alien—as foreigner—is addressed by Helen Kim in poems about immigrants/emigrants. Virginia beth Shields' graffiti work describes a woman of mixed race trying to define herself. Judy Kravis shows us existential anxiety in interpersonal relationships and within the family. Tension between the sexes is metaphorized in Michael Lunney's eerie fairy tale, *The History of Misogyny.* A memoir by William Wilson depicts the fragile border between the physically well and the dying, between the remembered past and the present. Two very different dream sequences by William Pope and Frigyes Karinthy as translated by Rachel Mikos-Naft lead us on a journey to displacement from self. Poems by Kevin Young, Janet Kaplan, Judy Bloomfield, and Star Black treat the alienation that comes from being lost in media and culture, a crime victim, betrayed by one's own body, and feeling trapped in any world.

What period of life is more alienating than adolescence? In fiction by Paul Lisicky and Cullen Gerst, teen-age protagonists—a gay heavy-metal lover in the burbs and a wisecracking babe on the streets of San Francisco—struggle to retain control of their souls. The coherent identity of Chester Freeman's narrator is in the balance when he's confronted by his mother's new boyfriend. Christine Liotta's fish-girl-woman returns to the water to save her life. And Denise Duhamel gives us a war bulletin from the border between childhood and puberty.

PATRICIA CHAO, JENNIFER COKE, *and*
KAREN DE BALBIAN VERSTER
Issue Editors

Name

by Virginia beth Shields

he calls her LAUNDRESS
he calls her REDDISHBROWNSKINAQUALINENOSESTR-
AIGHTBLACK HAIR

he calls her his subject this object
of the cultural anthropologist

he calls her aLmost WHITE
he calls her aLmost RED

whatever suits him at that particular time whatever
he takes a notion to whatever
he needs her to be

he even calls her CUNNING
When she tries to climb
out of the blood red soil that keeps her
in poverty

but not even Clorox or her strongest lYE SOAP
will take THAT STAIN out
and let her blend into the white stripes
of the American fabric

She calls her HOUSEKEEPER
when she looks between my Legs
my first gynecologist wonders aloud
why the skin   is so YELLOW
if I don't have CIRRHOSis of the LiveR when I tell her
my indian great-gRandmotheRs conspiRE
with the SUMMER SUN   to make me
this color   it is a trick
that I   ENjoY

She scoffs   telling me

YOU ARE NOT AN INDIAN
She Knows

She has ONE OF THEM
that cleans her house

it is my problem   she tells me

that I eat too many orange-colored root plants

she calls me SWEET POTATO EATER
and tells me

she'll see me lookin' whiter in 6 months

I'm already PALE as a SHEET
WHITE as a MAGGOT SHINY as WHITE MONEY
exsept in the Summertime when the
Sun warmS my SICKLY thin veiny Skin
to Such

a markedly different color
that I have to exSplain mySelf

I got a Wide latitude I tell 'em

I'm one of mY MAMAS PEOPLE
down South up north
I'm as WHITE AS MY DADDY

they call her CLAYEATER REDLEGSBRASS-
ANKLES PRETTY HAIR AND MUCH

MUCH WORSE
when she don't fit into a box
that they understAND

they do not call her MOTHER
they do not call her GRANDMOTHER
they do not call her anything
that would make her human

   they call her what they Have to I reckon
   to cover up
    what they do to her
   everyday

   and they must never
   let her
name herself

The History of Misogyny

by Michael Lunney

I ORDER THE SCRAMBLED EGGS WITH BUTTERED toast and black coffee at the Riverside Diner. There's no waitress to take my order and there isn't a river around for damn near two hundred miles. Oh, there had been—but our very own Whalen River is now just a sad, muddy ditch, snaking through our quiet, little town. And of course no waitress has ever worked the Riverside Diner.

It's October—the 14th of October. It hasn't rained in almost three years and all the chickens are dead. Now, a chicken is a stupid thing and you may not give a good goddamn—but these scrambled eggs are gonna cost me nine damn dollars and fifty-seven goddamn cents.

"Hey, what about my toast?" I ask the counterjohnny. "Says here I got some toast comin'. So…where is it? Where in hell—"

"But, James," young Billy Croker politely interrupts, "just who would you have turn this bread into toast?"

(Oddly enough, toast is believed to be something of a sacrament here at the Riverside Diner.)

"Listen," I say, "you barber-shaven white-handed sweet-mouthed tear-stained son-of-a-priest, my very own father made me toast every day of my young life—and he's the *only* man who ever called me James."

Ah well. Please understand that our friend Billy has always dreamt of praying for the souls of us men lost to the Whalen, as *he* played Mr. Jesus to a crowd of old women. But, hey—there's no longer a Whalen to be lost to and we…well, we can all be found right here at the Riverside Diner.

So I'm sitting with my coffee and I'm thinking about the woman I pulled from the Whalen last February. (And if you're wondering whether a river that hasn't tasted rain in over two years can safely support a woman: well, it can't. Though I myself didn't consider that till it was too late.)

It all happened a bit past dark on a Sunday night in late winter. I'd been alone on the river for most of that day. My nets were still down but what I was doing could hardly be called work. And I guess I'd been drinking a bit of the whiskey but I don't remember being too worried about it. I'd been pulling light nets for weeks and I knew my time on the Whalen was about over.

But when I hauled in my nets that dark winter night—and I remember wishing there was a moon to light the dangerous and dying river—I could feel the dead weight, the strange burden of my catch. I cursed the whiskey. I needed to be sober.

I *knew* what I had, and so I went to work on the nets. It was more than ten minutes before I reached her. Most times, they'll fight the net—but this one hadn't moved. I touched the side of her throat and I felt its fast beat. She wouldn't look at me, and I tried to turn her face with my hands. I was shamed by her nakedness, by her white skin. Did she want a blanket to cover herself? She said nothing. And I wondered if it was not her lament that I'd been sailing towards these past nights. (Perhaps she'd been trying to pass herself off as a mermaid—the only thing was, she couldn't croon worth a damn).

I was a tired drunk on a cold night—but this was my work. This is what I'd been raised for. And what I did that night should surprise no one.

I had to decide but I couldn't get a good look at her—and so finally it was the fact that her eyes seemed to be set rather curiously close together that persuaded me to toss her back. And as I clung to the rail and she fell to the river, I thought I heard her cry out. But I was wrong. It wasn't *she* who had wailed.

Now please don't believe that I'd ever given a second thought to these women. I'd worked the Whalen River for forty-one years and I'd made that very same decision perhaps twenty times before. And though it was a decision that was never easily come to (and I have seen the hardest men on this river quietly weep as they dropped a woman into the cold green and black waters of the Whalen), it was something that once done must be forgotten.

So I told myself and so I was told. But this past spring, while everyone sat in the Riverside Diner and waited for the rain that did not come, I sailed for weeks after the last boat had been put up.

And they said, "Jimmy, what the hell you lookin' for, Jimmy?"

"Well, goddamn," I said, "don't I remember telling you this story—"

"But Jimmy," they said, "we know you…and we've known you all your life. And you would risk nothing for a woman. Not your life, Jimmy. And not your boat."

But I was an old man with an old boat. And I was haunted by her. Haunted by how she'd been so calm and still as I carried her to the rail, and how she wouldn't look at me and how I'd lifted her to that rail and only then—as I let her drop—had she opened her eyes. And I would always remember that, as I would remember how she'd hit the water and that she didn't cry out as the others always had, but went silently under.

"But the Whalen is dead, Jimmy," they said, "and everybody knows it—"

And I knew it. But I preferred working the shallow dead water of the Whalen River to sitting over all-day refills of cool black coffee at the Riverside Diner. And that, as you can see, was coming soon enough…

Now my coffee is cold and I'm counting out my pennies (as I don't want to over tip this bastard of a counterjohnny, who has the nasty habit of stabbing me in the back with rusty forks), when I feel this tugging at my leg. And here, in the Riverside Diner, is the smallest man I've ever seen.

"Buddy," he says, "Buddy, if you could help a guy onto a stool, he would be much obliged."

Hell, this man doesn't weigh much more than a wet beagle pup. He orders coffee (light with three sugars). He asks if a man can find work.

I say, "This is a river town—"

"With no river," he says. "I understand. I know the Whalen—I worked her tugs as a young man."

His voice is calm and his hands are sturdy—but he *must* be hungry. I've just blown my last sawbuck on scrambled eggs and so I stand and say: "Hey! Who here wants to buy a hungry man lunch?" And Johnny McGuire up and bets his poor ol' grandmum's dentures that nobody will take me up on it.

"Well now," Luke Martin says, "don't young Johnny always seem to be puttin' the smart money down. And may God help and save you, Jimmy—but McGuire here already owns your eyes (I'd lost my glasses to Johnny McGuire several months earlier when he challenged my insistence that we still bothered to bury our dead)—and here you are trying to give him your teeth, boy."

I started to get nervous. Mr. Martin (who, some fifty years ago, swore to my dying father that he'd watch out for me) knew us well. And he says, "We've never liked strangers here at the Riverside Diner." He stops to swallow some coffee (black with rye whiskey) and do a little thinking. "Hell, Jimmy—we don't like *ourselves* too goddamn much."

Yes, we're ugly men and we're drunks and we've never learned to be kind. We like to work but our work is mean. And may Jesus Christ have mercy on us, for we're poor vicious bastards and our beloved Whalen River is dead.

So, yeah, I'd say McGuire has himself a pretty darn good bet going. But the small man wants no part of it. He doesn't look at me and he doesn't look at McGuire or anyone else, but only nods to the counterjohnny, who brings him a refill on the coffee.

And it's then that she walks in, a pale young woman with dark glasses and tangled black hair. She sits at the counter on the other side of the small man. The counterjohnny brings her coffee (light, no sugar) without her asking. She must've been sitting in the Riverside Diner all morning, alone in the back room (where one can see what remains of the once-mighty Whalen River—which is why we pitiful men always crowd into the front).

There is an awkward pause and a silence, as young women are just not to be seen in the Riverside Diner. We mostly know women from our work and, though we've loved them terribly, those beautiful women that we've sometimes lured from the Whalen River…they've always come to despise us.

She turns to the small man and says, "I am a stranger here myself."

And that man lifts his cup but he does not speak.

"What I mean is…I would like to buy you lunch."

"Thank you," he says, "but I'm just having coffee."

"Please," she says softly (and I believe that only I can hear this part), "I know what it is to be hungry."

"What I really need is work," he says. "I have children and I have a wife and I have parents—"

"Do you work the rivers?"

"Yes," he says.

"The work will return."

And I'm thinking, what the *h e l l*—I mean, what was *that* all about? What can this woman know about our work and what does she mean by saying that it will return to us?

But the small man seems to understand all this well enough, for he takes up his cup, jumps down from his seat, and follows the woman into the back room of the Riverside Diner. But for Mr. Martin, they all follow.

Mr. Martin pulls on his coat.

"Where are you going?" I ask.

"Where are *you* going?"

"Nowhere," I say.

"All right, then," he says. And he begins to walk slowly toward the front door.

"Mr. Martin—wait."

"Yes."

"What do you make of all this?"

"What?"

"Well, this woman—"

"This woman is beautiful, boy," he says. "Please don't believe she could ever do anything but hurt us."

He walks away.

And I promise myself that I will not let Mr. Martin go unburied—that I will use the grave that my father intended for me.

I turn toward the back room. And it is there, in that long-silent room overlooking the sad precipice, that the pale young woman shouts to that bastard of a counterjohnny for some hotcakes with maple syrup, and plenty of toast, and some juice—and we need more coffee here!

He carries his tall order back to his counter and I can see him there, bent over a block of clean blond wood, cutting bread. And then I turn to watch Billy Croker, who has already closed his eyes and dropped to his knees....

He begins to quietly petition the Lord for the undeserved grace necessary to transform, by his all-consuming fire, what appears to be week-old bread into toast.

But before Billy can even begin the catalogue of our sins-to-be-forgiven, the toast comes...and the hotcakes come and some juice and the coffee and lots of jam...and when the pale young woman is busted by the fourth stack of cakes, we are shamed into tossing a few coins into Billy Croker's hat—hell, even that bastard McGuire throws in his two bits.

And graciously I thank him and I'm telling him to please just forget about the dentures (figuring that the ol' crone probably has a mouth to match her fool grandson's, anyway), when Joseph walks into the diner.

Here at the Riverside Diner, we *know* Joseph. We know that at the tender age of two months, his kind—but farsighted—grand-mother mistook him to be an unripe summer squash and that he spent (it is said) the saddest part of a week in a vegetable bin.

Joseph hears us in the back and walks through the diner to find us. And when he comes into the room (we are, at this time, gathered about our new friend, who is eating a slice of sacred rye toast), only the woman turns to see.

Joseph goes straight to the window. He has comes to tell us something.

"Is it the rain?" she asks.

But Joseph—Joseph cannot speak.

Documents

by Frigyes Karinthy

(translated by Rachel Mikos-Naft)

Frigyes Karinthy (1887 – 1938) was described by one commentator as being as central to literary life in Budapest as Aristophanes was to Athens. He seems to be remembered today in Hungary primarily as a humorist, but as the following short story shows, he was deeply committed to exploring, in an often eerily prescient way, the wrenching dilemmas of twentieth-century modernity—a territory he shares with Kafka, to be sure, but to which he contributes his own very unique satirical twist, as well as the ineffable sense of a lone shattered voice denouncing the hypocrisy of totalizing systems.

AT THAT VERY MOMENT, I WAS ALREADY FEELING that there was going to be a problem of some kind—that there was something I'd forgotten, that I needed to make some move, shout, or struggle somehow—because if I didn't, I would never be able to wake up again.

So that at that very moment when the dream began—this, the most dreadful of my dreams—I still was aware that it was just a dream. And yet I knew just as well that if I slept for even just one more minute, I'd never be able to wake up again—I'd never be able to tell that it was only a dream.

I could still move, then: could still stretch my legs, my hands out in front of me—yes, I was on a great field, there were mountains all around me, and the sun shone brightly. And if I wanted to see the sun for myself, I turned my head upward of my own free will—and if I got tired, I sat down, and if I wanted to go somewhere, I stood up.

But even then I was already feeling, with a kind of chilling, lethal premonition, that there was something I'd forgotten. This forgotten *something* was going to lead to a big problem, I felt—I had to go somewhere, and at that somewhere, say something; I had to turn up at someone's door, where they would know all about me—things I didn't in the least bit know. But I had completely forgotten all of these worries, because it was so good to lie in the grass, to look up and reflect upon that great blue sphere, which rocked me and life in the happy infinity of emptiness.

I began to feel, with a nagging anxiety, that I had better not turn onto the road: I was afraid I might bump into someone. I went across the hill, and then I saw a policeman—he stood before a little cottage. It looked like he was guarding the hill, so that no one would take it. My heart constricted with anxiety, but I turned my face into a blank, expressionless mask—seeing as I had to pass in front of him—because it would have seemed too suspicious, had I turned around. It would have seemed suspicious, and the last thing I could afford to do was to arouse suspicion—because I had forgotten something, and I had no way of knowing what it was, this forgotten *something*, and which I was sure they already knew about. Was it some hideous offense? I calculated that I would overtake the policeman in about twenty paces: I'll walk right along, I told myself, I won't even look at him: he'll see for himself I have nothing to fear. I'll whistle a little tune, I won't turn around, and I won't hurry my steps, no matter how my irregularly, convulsively beating heart urges, presses me on. I shall proceed as if my pulse were beating at a completely normal rate—just like the doctor always orders. Then maybe he won't notice me.

That's exactly what I did, as I walked along: I whistled softly, I didn't look his way. But I could feel him looking at me: I slowed my steps, went more slowly and more slowly: this was my downfall. He thought I wanted to stop; I heard him calling after me. Twice I pretended not to hear him, but by the third time I knew I couldn't keep that up any longer. I stopped, and turned around.

—Where are you going?

I told him some fiction.

—What is your name?

I felt myself in the grip of a lethal fear—for this was it, the thing I'd forgotten. I approached him and hurriedly, excitedly, began to explain that surely this was not important, what my name was, but that surely the fact that here I stood, with one head and two legs, a living and moving human being: that surely this was proof enough of my existence. I protested passionately that I remembered everything with great exactitude: my earliest childhood, the picture-books, my mother, my father, and that I had been born in a completely normal fashion, like any other person, or living thing: that I differed in no way from anyone else, and was as little worthy of being addressed as whatever blade of grass here on the field. I wanted to mislead him, to distract him, make him start talking about something else, about the nature all around us: I thought that was clever. But it turned out to be all in vain, and a horrified scream formed in my throat, because I saw his hand stretching out towards me.

—That's all very nice, he said, and he put his hand on my shoulder—but a name is absolutely necessary. You cannot go on without it.

—So give me some name, and let me go.

The policeman looked at me with great injury, and assured me that he was an honorable and decent man; that he knew his duties and obligations; that he hardly had claim to such a task; and that it would all be for the best if I spoke of it no more. If all of my affairs were in good order, I would have nothing to fear; that he himself would accompany me to the Record Office of the Fourth District Division of Registries. There, they would be able to find out who I was. It would be much better if I didn't resist, because then he would be obligated to take the matter to the Assistant Clerkship of Inquiries and Reconnaissance, and the whole thing would take much longer there.

So I didn't resist, I went with him, and as we went along I wildly strained to figure out within myself what I was going to say; I felt more and more flustered.

Dusk began to fall.

We were walking along a street with many, many houses—I looked at the windows, and I peeked in between the houses eagerly, to see if I could catch a glimpse of the Danube; but the streets only opened up onto other streets, and the uniformly, regularly shaped windows lined up in rows of three and four very tidily, like soldiers. We went through a gate, into a square courtyard, then came, unexpectedly, onto a series of long corridors—a heavy odor of brick dust struck my nasal passage, and did not leave. Down in the courtyard workers were hammering, sawing, building things and painting—horses, hitched up to wagons, were hauling off huge cartloads of quarry dust. Above all the sight of a low and dark corridor, in which gas lamps were hissing, was frightening to me: we turned into this corridor and opened a door, from which charts and tables dangled in profusion. Within the room gas lights were also burning: on the tall counters, pillars of paper, all at least one meter tall, lay scattered about, covering the entire surface. The walls were lined with cubbyholes, made of lengthwise and crosswise wooden planks. Above each cubbyhole, there was a letter. While the policeman chatted with a yellow and grey person, I gnawingly looked at these letters, and in thought I softened them: I drew more flexibly, more compliantly the relentless straight lines of A and H; and above the gallows tree of T, I drew useless and beautiful arabesques.

A hoarse and colorless voice called out to me to wait, and a yellow, paper-faced clerk went up a ladder. He pulled out a great mass of documents, put them on his shoulder and climbed down. I began to feel that I was suffocating, and meekly, with a pale smile, I asked if I could go out onto the street while they looked for the document. He responded that this would not be possible until eight o'clock at night, and that by then it would be already dark.

So I waited, and I tried to look as pale and as sickly as the pile of dossiers I was leaning up against: perhaps one way to go unobserved. Someone lit a gas lamp, and an ink-spotted hand rummaged grumblingly in the stack of documents. Thirty-two, thirty-three—he muttered, and suddenly stopped.

—37321—said the clerk.—The preregistration form isn't in the folder, and the district heading isn't stamped. You shouldn't be here; you have to go to Protocol.

He wrote something with a red pencil on the document, stamped it, moistened his finger, stuck a red slip of paper onto it, then put it into my hand. I started down the corridor, and suddenly, I noticed the doors—they were getting smaller and smaller, and sinking deeper and deeper into the walls. A heavy odor of must and paper rose up, acidic blotting paper, indelible ink, and glue. A shadow glided by me on the wall, turned and then harshly called out:

—What do you want?

—Protocol…I stammered.

—This way.

I stumbled into a room-like cavity, across three staircases—in the depths there stood tables, piles of documents as tall as towers,

cubbyholes. Yellow, uniformly mole-faced, grey-haired crea-
tures moved uniformly, in even measure. Someone took the document from my hand, and hurriedly began to write on it. Then,
without turning to me:

—Hair? he asked.

—Of uncertain color…I said.

—Eyes?…Mouth?…Eyebrows?

I wanted to answer, but my previous reply stuck in my throat.
The clerk more and more hurriedly, more and more demandingly
began to grill me.

—Head?…Hands?…Nerves?…Legs?

I lost my head, I felt that my end was close at hand, I
swooned. I wanted to run towards the windows, but they seized
me. I felt cold fingers on my throat, I squirmed, tears came to
my eyes, but at once they dried up again: someone was blotting
my face with blotting paper. I could see nothing.

—He shouldn't be here—said a voice—The preregistration
form is missing from Dossier 37321, it has to be countersigned.
Take him to the Third Bureau of the Reference Office, have
them give him an envelope, and get him into the Registry. In
four months, they can show him the door, signed, sealed and
delivered. The thing is that he not get lost.

I felt a heavy blow on my temple: as if I'd been struck with
some kind of stamp. Then I heard the hurried rustling of papers,
and footsteps rang out. Someone picked me up and carried me.

—Be very careful: you are responsible for him! said a voice—
He must be registered.

—What should I do with his blood? asked a second voice.

—Pour it into a glass, number it, and send it to the warehouse.

Again the busy rustling of papers. I felt my blood turning
cold; I heard the dumb whoosh of a stopper, as if they were
pulling it out of me somewhere. Then, from above, across my

mouth, as I opened it to scream, I felt a cold and foul liquid being poured in: ink. My veins filled up with this liquid, then everything settled and dried, windingly, throughout my entire body. They blotted dry this circuitous pattern; a hand smoothed me, flattened me out.

A second hand, knotty and gnarled, wrote something on me, then stamped me: by now it no longer hurt. They picked me up; now I was as light as a feather, almost completely transparent: they folded me in two, and put me in the envelope. I heard footsteps shuffling on the ladder—then it was dark, and in one of the cubbyholes, a hand glided me in between two documents, and let fall onto me the rest.

And now here I wait, my God, here I've been waiting for years, amidst the dusty, musty papers, the grey layers of dust. Here I wait, and I nurse, I coddle the dull torment of my bestamped, bethrottled brain: perhaps there is yet some strength, though, in this decayed suffering—that after long, long years, the papers thronging, pressing round me will light up and burn—that one day everything shall burst into flames, the yellow sheets shall whirl around in circles in a red fire-tempest, and the swirling breeze shall cast me out, burning and sooty, but free, forward towards the clouds, across and above the fields: as light, as ethereal, as flying ashes—upon which nothing can be written anymore.

Or the decay itself shall simply crumble; within a hundred years we shall all crumble to dust, my poor, poor, papery colleagues. Then only a tiny breeze shall suffice to be lifted out the window, to quietly be deposited on the sands between the puny blades of grass. And grass shall come of it again, within a hundred years, or perhaps again a human being…Or shall it still be as dust, sterile even when mixed within the sands, barren and eternally dead—the accursed dust of documents?

Cacti and Succulents

by Judy Kravis

*...there are profound mysteries in a Real Cactus Soil which no
cactus maniac would betray, even if you broke him on the wheel.
All these sects, observances, rituals, schools and lodges, as well as
the wild or hermit cactus maniacs, will swear that only by their
Method alone have they achieved such miraculous results.*

WE EYE EACH OTHER FROM A SHORT, SPIKY DISTANCE.
What difficult secret do we share? We hardly want to know but
we keep looking, and the middle distance fills with cacti and
succulents we have known. Our encounters usually take place
under the cover of something else. We should be talking about
literature but we're talking about the rare varieties you can
sometimes find in supermarkets, and how you might not really
know what they are till they flower. Other people indulge our
conversation for a moment then leave us in our thicket of
strange forms, by the checkout.

How far back does this go? A long way, usually to childhood.
We grew cacti from seed by the age of ten. Every day over an
entire winter and a spring we pulled out the box from under the
living room sofa, and one day we knew the crystal of dust that
was a pinpoint of *mammillaria* in a sea of John Innes No. 1 com-
post. Two weeks later an *opuntia*. Or was it a *lithops*? Already we
saw the eleven-inch star-shaped flower the *stapelia variegata*
would have one day, purply-black with gold markings, and the
sky-eating white of the *epiphyllium*. The Latin was proof of ele-
gance, enigma and things that don't move.

Cacti and succulents were part of civilisation. Their aureoles of spines, their clusters of hooked hairs left an itch that was hard to locate. They were mysteriously alive, inscrutably contained, the ones that looked like stones or sausages, the ones that spat their young off the ends of spotted stalks, their ears, bracts, entire forms masquerading as leaves. You could take cuttings and one day see a new green sausage fill with light. Bits that fell off would grow. They came from the desert and the jungle, they were parched, replete and on your windowsill, the face you turned to the outside world, lapping the slender small-town sun.

A cactus is a succulent, sub- of a genus, member of a family, butt of a joke if not beyond one. The prickles are there to remind you. A cactus becomes a succulent when it loses its prickles, and vice versa. Are you with me? Some people find cacti unbearably enigmatic, and succulents irritating. So many fleshy leaves off a like-minded stem, so few reluctant flowers. That disinterestedness of the born skeptic. You can ignore a cactus, can't you, leave it in the window for years? You don't need to water them more than once a year, if that, they're reservoirs aren't they? Ships of the ships of the desert, last ditch for desert rats. If ignored they will prosper, and may even let out a rare, astounded blossom, the sudden riot of life almost more than you can bear, the background music Beethoven, a cactus if ever you heard one.

You can't ignore a cactus, can you? You have become one.

Don't judge me by my spots, you say, rather, by my spikes. I'm awkward in a crowd but can hold a windowsill single-handed. Generic desert all around me. An isolationist. A reservoir. Groups of us can portray a gawky charm. We like to be plunged to the neck in gravel and watered indirectly. We agree to tell all and we tell nothing. We try for a south-facing aspect. The world could end and we'd still be there, inviolate. You begin to guess that there's no such thing as normal and we're proof of it, cacti and succulents, members and friends. Like mayflies in May and mushrooms on St. George's Day, we're reliable and unaccountable, scattered about in shops, houses, offices, in a habit of light in a gap between net curtains.

Was it that first propagation under the living-room sofa? Or the first visit to the greenhouses at Kew? Or having a greenhouse of your own? Or when you were given your first cutting by Jimmie, the first cactus fancier you knew? A moment whereafter you felt a bolt of recognition at the sight of a fellow, an absentee in a window, like Emma Bovary—an underwatered succulent if ever there was one.

Jimmie was soft and slightly withdrawn. She looked at you from far back, her hands on the staging in the conservatory in front of a large, dusty, nameless plant with a crock of red-pink flowers. Was she looking at you or just taking you in on her way through? The glass on the conservatory mossy within and milky without. She leaned back as she told you the name in Latin and the habit of the plant. Downy, with fine, hooked hair. Straight fringe, wide face; between a smile and a daze, stooped shoulders in a big frame. Jimmie was one of The Girls, three women who ran a small-holding, a café and a Jersey cow. Girls of a feather. Jimmie was the horticultural Girl, Eileen looked after the animals, Mollie ran the café. Eileen was a cactus, Mollie a succulent. Jimmie was epileptic.

Members of the Society of Cacti and Succulents, and Friends, take heed: there are more of us than you know, we're lodged on all manner of shelf and saucer, usually far from the window which may well face North. Sometimes we're watered too indirectly. A glance round the door. Mist through an open window on a summer evening. We might not be watered at all. We might search high and low. We might not be able to move.

Then the cactus maniacs begin to shout all together, and attack one another with their fists, teeth, hooves and claws; but as is the way of this world, the real truth is not brought to light even by these means.

An Aunt is Free

by Judy Kravis

THE NEW AUNT HAS NOT BEEN AND WILL NOT BE A MOTHER.

The old aunt was gruff and autocratic, a pseudo-man with soft patches in a piercing look; she kept dogs and good works, bristling and barking and coming up trumps with cash or scones. The new aunt works through fourteen different catalysts, slips on fourteen thousand suits and slips out again. She might do ballet or Tai Chi. Hands grab from the balcony: here, try this one, this one is You. She wakes up startled that the sleep wasn't hers, only the silence. She may well play Wagner at three a.m. The food she eats is off-beam and photogenic. Girl children look at her with curiosity. Between the new aunt and the old aunt came the romantic, unreal, traveling-raveling aunt who had love affairs and secret purpose and was rarely seen, even in books; a part-time aunt, like the American uncle but less munificent, even more vague, with untidy luggage and jet lag. You did not have to meet one to know one, you could imagine them in hotels all over the world, on esoteric business, with unexplained debility, unkempt passions, playing the cello or the stock exchange. The life of the romantic aunt is a catalogue of opportunity offered and invented, a spectacle of competence and high adventure: she garbles and gallivants, she decamps, she overnights, she lives alone and has skirmishes from which she emerges, you'd think, lightly grazed.

I'm a new aunt of twenty-one years standing. I've come of age. I've done time as an old aunt, preserving fruit and writing poetry; I've done eccentric travel and skirmishes, including some full-scale wars. The new aunt is a true aunt now. My auntish freedom has already deterred a couple of mothers, and drawn from others a mother-free persona. I have two nephews and a niece whom I rarely see or hear from. I have hindered being useful to them by moving to another island where for the bulk of my aunthood I have maintained a complex frontal system of old, new and romantic aunts, childless, dogless and difficult to know.

It came to me on the bus—you can be haunted on a bus as nowhere else, as the thin rumble of a diesel engine rushes up your spine, glacé on the 347 heading north-west—I did what I was told. An aunt gets her instruction early: Hear thou, thou shalt do better than I did, thou shalt not make my mistake, and for that thou shalt go free, on thine own two feet thou shalt go, and stay, out of (a mother's) trouble. The bus lurches to a stop. It could be the Hotel Terminus; it could have a 40 watt bulb in the hall, you could have lived there all your life, in your auntish prison. You sit there, frozen in your seat as the bus turns round, you'll pay your fare again. You won't go home, you'll go visit friends and the girl children will finger your hair, wanting to hear what you ate the day before, how much of it you grew, what oddness you have perpetrated on the ordinary world, what revenge. You're knowledgeable about plants aren't you, you take cuttings, collect seeds from the gardens of friends. You devour the view from the terrace, their view the more obstinately yours now. A glass of honeysuckle champagne and your feet propped up on a low wall. The staggering peace of other people's lives, the matchless exactitude of their houses and gardens. You love them all. The curtains bellying slightly out from the draw-ing-room. Grand piano, why not? Large, no longer fragrant bowl of potpourri. Strangely formal freedom; newly disquieting lines of fire and lines of recollection.

This is what an aunt does, this is what she knows, her secret imperialism, the great range of her short sight. It isn't the Hotel Terminus, it's the Hotel du Lac. As mothers into grandmothers, so aunts into great-aunts deliquesce. We start to need a formal garden, by god, with all that freedom fermenting in our brain. Pass me my mantle, Jerome, I'll wear the Leghorn today.

Queens, New York

by Helen Kim

Mia was fat
not a typical Asian;
slim and slender
to her finger tips.
She sat on the stoop
under a fluorescent light

crying, 'the knife, just
playing around, you know.'
Her thick accent lodged
on the lips. The white cop
sticks out Michael's finger.
Blood dripping from
his Black skin.
'Jealous, he's jealous,'
the fat girl screams.

'We have laws in this land,
no domestic violence, understand?'
The white cop handcuffs her wrists.
The fat girl's eyes disappear
under the fat lids again.
Tears drop like the way
her mother once described,
big as chicken eggs when she was hungry.

'Michael, please tell them, please.'
Michael slinks away,
'I ain't gonna take no shit
from no chink no mo.'
The glass door flashes
her image and closes.
'No one. I don't have no one.'
The fat girl wails as the white cop
pushes her head down
into the cavern of the blue car.

Reunion

by Helen Kim

My cousin's new born baby girl,
half Korean, placed fragilely among us,
half crazed half blinded people. In
whose tongue the bitter taste
of Japanese words still remain. In
whose blood the sound of bombs
still explode on the dirt road
leading from Seoul, 1953.

1993, New Jersey. In a room
full of glittering frames
and a high tech Karaoke system
we sing along, clapping, laughing,
blotting out each other's voices.

Have we forgotten so quickly
the sorrow of leaving the divided body?
First in half, then into many pieces?

The motes of our memory float in the room
across the screen and a Monet copy
lodging in this cousin or that uncle
then in the eyes of the baby girl
whose cry drowns among the singing.

The Slut

by Cullen Gerst

CLETO WAS COMING ON TO ME WHILE I WAS STILL living with my mom. I don't blame him for wanting some. My mom isn't hella old for a mom, actually she's only 37, which means she had me when she was twenty-one, major mistake-o. Still, she deserves a little more, despite the fact she walks around like she's the only one in the Milky Way having good sex, the sass of that bitch. Her man Cleto the massage therapist who sells Herbalife and whatever, who supplies her with reliably emotional sex I gather. I'm the kind of bitch that does not give a fuck. I let him go down on me two times, three if you count the one through my jeans during the earthquake under the table.

Maybe I shouldn't have. I shouldn't have. Now he's El Conquistador and tries to get a feel every time my mom's not looking. I was already coming for like a whole year, although his position as current boyfriend of my mother did lend a certain edge to the experience.

It gets gross, when he looks like Carlos Santana. It gets gross then, believe me. Funky-ass beads around his neck, glass I think. That thing he's doing all mayonnaise. I don't know why anyone would want to do that. His shit is broke off, and I'll say that to his face.

My mother has pitiful life. She makes these humungous salads that mean let's be a family now, now we can love each other, now we can say anything to each other. The salads always have lots of cheese and healthy lettuce, the organic kind, and pine nuts or other nuts, and asparagus which I hate, and tuna and halved tomatoes, cherry kind, which I also hate, and it's so healthy it makes you sick.

Anyway. She was all, eat this salad and smile at me, smile for all the fucked up things I do, smile because of how lonely I am. She's got that look on her face. I'm happy I hope you're happy too, Mina. I'm going bullshit. Join me, be like me, smile and eat my salad. Okay, I will never be like her. God someone shoot me the second that shit happens, I'm serious.

We sit down to gorge on this stupid bowl of salad, and she's already not too too happy with me because this was when I changed my name to Petrolea for a while. She didn't cream when I got my piercing either, which basically shows she has no respect for who I am. She's the one always telling me to be myself.

I walk up behind Cleto, who's smacking his lips and has a piece of sprout stuck to the cleft in his chin, and ram my tongue down his ear, okay? I stick my tongue in his ear and we go, we talk, we shout, my mom's upset let's put it that way. The password is ballistic.

I take my hand and run it over his crotch, which I choose for irony's sake since it's right out of his repertoire, and all of a sudden he's got to go, he forgot an appointment. You can see the outline of his boner through his 1979 booty-ass Le Chic designer jeans and whatever.

She's mad she says, I'm a slut she says. I decide to talk about the truth and whatever. I go, Who's had about twenty-nine boyfriends in the last five years, who's the slut now? Cleto suggests that we not talk about this now, that in his Group they postpone anger to resolve difference, that everyone now, be quiet, everyone now. But my mom and I agree that we should talk about this now. I can see it in your eyes, she says to Cleto.

Tell me, she says, and Cleto tells her. About how I seduced him. Fucking lies. How many times? my darling mother asks and does her nervous thing with her fingers and her mouth. Once. That's a fat fucking lie, I respectfully add. Twice. Liars are always lying.

As if he was only a bystander who found himself innocently staring into a vagina, Cleto jumps in with how I was the one who wanted to. Your repartee is pitiful, I go. I'm in beginning French class, which I still go to when the teacher isn't being an asshole.

This is when my mom drags the casserole across his face. She's crying a lot even for her, which is saying something because it doesn't take much for her to muster up a few wet ones. She's a total master. This time it won't work, as much as she thinks it will. I can't live in her house anymore, I know. Get out of my house, in fact, were her exact words I think. I go, Don't waste your breath, it's not like I need your encouragement. Shit.

Then she's all, I betrayed her and she'll never recover herself and that I hurt her. Shit. How could I when I knew she was going through menopause? Her self-esteem is not what she hoped it would be by now and whatever. Look, I'll just go around the corner and live with my dad.

I hear he's got a girlfriend that's a real slut. I'll fit right in. Do you think he'll be a little happy to see me? do you think he loves me a little? do you think I even care about you? Funky ass bitch.

What did you call me, what did you say?

I said you were a bitch because you're acting like a little bitch, which is what you are.

I had to leave pretty quick after that. On the stairs I heard my mother ask Cleto how come he never does that for her. Do you know what upsets me most of all? What upsets me most of all is that you don't do that for me.

Shit. Who would want to? you couldn't pay someone to. Probably have to get a shot after at the Free Clinic. Probably funky as sour milk, I can't really blame Cleto. I hope mine won't ever be old like hers. As I ran through the hall my mother shouted not to come back crying. I said don't wait up for me, I said why don't you leave the light on. I can be hella saucy sometimes, usually I'm shyer though.

Slamming the door, I go three steps towards the gate and she's on the porch crying. She goes, you can always come back Mina. Be careful. If you want me you know where I am.

Did she mistake me for someone who gives a fuck? It's so easy to act guilty when you're her. She stretches her arms out as I walk away, the whole enchilada. The neighbors watching from their porches are impressed by this but I'm not. I think I might have been dumb to leave my mom's house. Two times this week Cleto's tried to follow me. But I carry a tear gas canister called The Terminator, okay? And I got a fourteen-inch-long knife with a snakeskin handle that I got off a dead guy in the park, and I can get a nine if I need it. If he comes after me again, he'd better pray, and that's all I got to say. It won't be my fault.

That was last week. Now I kick it practically every day, either at my homey's house or on Telegraph. Today I'm on Telegraph. No one can make me do anything. If you go to Telegraph you might see me there. The first thing you would notice about me is that I have kind of big lips for a white girl. I don't like them but boys do. You can tell them if they want blowjobs to forget about it. I also talk to myself, but I only do it when people aren't around. It's weird when you talk to yourself. I don't know the person I talk to when I talk to myself. I think I might be dumb or weird.

I saw my brother Ajai this morning. This is how he goes: Buds, buds, doses, doses. He's looking good and whatever. He's a light-skinned because his mom was from Guyana. I think about her sometimes, she used to cook me and him pinto beans and crabs in cayénne when we were young. I want to live in Guyana, she told me about it. Anywhere is better than here. She died in a car accident.

She was unhappy, what are you going to do? She was like most people. I'm glad I didn't have to identify the body and whatever, like Ajai did. Her on the hood. Ajai changed a little after that and through his door I heard him crying.

He's a rad brother to have. He's been dropping sid since seventh grade practically, and when I talk shit he always says, I was way more hard than you when I was fourteen so don't give me no bullshit. His mother's old buddies, all these African dudes with red eyes, give him dank like every other week. We get zonked together.

I was totally into him like two years ago, okay? Since he was only my half-brother I didn't really see him all that much, and he was a little bit older than me, you know, brown legs, brown back with his shirt off. I was hella nervous around him. I used to have crazy-ass fantasies about him, he was the first guy I ever masturbated to. One time I farted accidentally when I was talking to him and our dad, and I almost died.

But now I'm out of that phase and we've been cool ever since. I'm not ashamed or anything because Ajai's hella fine and hella nice and all my friends agree with me. That boy is rooty tooty fresh and booty, I'm sorry. He's all good to himself. Buds, buds, doses, doses. That boy is the bomb.

But anyway. I saw him this morning and he says our dad wants to talk to me and whatever. He goes, Dad's going to be at Blondie's at one o'clock he wanted me to say. Oh word? I go.

He's high and starts to laugh, he likes to get high, so do I. Now first of all, what I said to my mom, one thing: I would never live with my dad, never. This is a man I've probably talked to more than, Tell me about school, Let me tell you about Vietnam, Let me tell you about your mother's evil ways, maybe zero times in my life.

He gets to see me one weekend every month. You're so God damned holy, dad, shit. I remember thinking, Fuck that, I want you two to fight over me. I want you to spend your life savings on lawyers. Hella compassionate look on his face: I'm trying to make this work, Mina, I know this will be hard. Sucker.

He used to sell some sort of vitamin-fortified fruit shake on Telegraph in the sixties. I don't know what it is, it's got algae in it or whatever. Now he's mass producing it, makes casual connections in San Francisco every day, has a modern house in the hills with a refrigerator and oven that are self-cleaning. The house is kind of tight, actually. That's basically how you can tell when someone is through, when they hang out in San Francisco. I don't understand how a man can have a son like Ajai, who is a total chiller, and not be a chiller himself. You are so liberal, dad, you are so caring, you are so through, you are so fucked.

You've got brass tree frogs in your garden, and you like to show people pictures of yourself in El Salvador but all you can think of to say is how cheap things are there. So now you want to know your daughter and make everything better, maybe you want to tell me I've grown up so fast and that you're proud. Don't make me spit in your face, you sellout.

I didn't want to go to Blondie's, but by one I was hella hungry. It's a quiet day for Telegraph. I walk by Blondie's and then, on accident, I go inside. I walk straight to the counter and order a slice of cheese and a coke, one-seventy-five. As I'm paying I feel him notice me. The change sticks in my hand, the dimes and nickels. I fold my slice the long way and try to cradle it on the tips of my fingers so the greasy wax paper doesn't burn me. I don't have to look up, I know where he's sitting. I pretend to be hella interested in a scrap of bubbling cheese on the crust of my slice.

Mina, How you doing comes his voice, and then an arm comes around my shoulder and squeezes, and for some reason I let it stay and I look up and go, Hi dad. He's got a lightly pressed collared shirt and whatever. He smells like incense and has a killer tan that makes him look younger than he is. His shiny brown hair is in a ponytail, not even falling out a little even though he's forty-two. Mine is bleached and I want his instead.

He's all, Thanks for coming, and I'm all, Yeah sure, so he knows not to waste my time being fluffy. He smiles when I say this, and it's a sad smile so I look out the front window. Some Mexicans are having a bottle fight out there. I go, Take me for a beer, this place sucks. He doesn't mind bottle fights, he says, meeting my eyes. I haven't seen his eyes in a year.

He was a big time tweeker back in the day. Before I was born. Big time. When I was like nine, one time I came into his apartment that he had with his new wife, the one from Guyana, and they were lighting up a spliff. He told me what they were doing wasn't bad enough not to do, but was bad enough not to tell anyone about.

Sitting there in Blondie's he's close to crying. He offers me a cigarette and as I take it I say out of the corner of my mouth, Good to see you're still smoking, dad. I call him dad because he always wanted his kids to call him just Tom. He wipes the sweat from his smooth brown forehead with his wrist and sighs. Then he takes one leg and with his hand crosses it over the other on his stool.

I go to myself, Oh shit here we go, and I kick at the legs of my stool and look at the pattern on the floor. Where have you been living lately? he asks. I go to myself, Good question dude. Say something. Say something good. What do you mean where am I living exactly? Shit, let him do the work, shit. I know you're not living with your mother, and he's all soft and breathy when he says mother. I go, you mean The Bitch. Yes, I mean The Bitch, if you want to call her that obviously I understand.

It's so soothing to know that you're keeping an eye on me since I am your only daughter and whatever.

I'm not used to saying I'm sorry, and I've never said it to you, Mina, but I am, I am truly sorry about the way things are between us. I want you to know that you can stay with me any-time. God, you don't know how hard this is. Have kids. Then you'll know.

I manage a smile just as pathetic as his and say no thanks.

I shrug. That's all I need to do. And I say, Don't humble your-self to me, don't be sorry, your life is pretty successful, I guess I understand.

Don't mumble, Mina, what did you say? please try to enunciate.

Now I look him in the eye just for a second and go, Nothing, but I know he heard every word. Now I wish I was in Guyana. His eyes are milky. He looks down at his slice, which he still hasn't touched, and shakes his head. He begins again, more tired.

Okay okay, I mean, have you been sleeping in the park, or dumpstering? This is crazy, do you live on Telegraph, Mina?

I nod vaguely and decide not to tell him. He's almost like a child, unsure of himself. I pull The Terminator out of my back-pack and say, just like the Marines have and I also got a fourteen-inch knife with a snakeskin handle, not bad for a white girl, huh? When I say this I feel something. I think it might be that I'm happy.

And what about school, or should I even ask, he grins. I grin too and go, Actually I go to class sometimes, which is true at least when it comes to French. I tell him I need to learn French so I can move to Guyana, which surprises him and he goes, Guyana? And I go, probably. He licks his lips and I see him casually think of his dead wife.

Do you have enough money? You must not eat much.

Be careful now, Mina, be very careful, I go to myself. Say something. Say something good. Then I'm all, No I don't really need anything. Sometimes ladies give me change when they come out of the Gap.

He goes, So you see Ajai anyway, and I can't help but laugh a little. When I search for more from him he says, You'll be glad, I suppose, to know that Ajai won't tell me anything about you.

Hell yeah, Ajai, I love you more than the world!

I don't suppose either it would do any good to tell you that the marijuana I used to smoke was not nearly as strong as the stuff you guys get now.

I shake my head: No, it would not do any good to say that. At this point I'm looking for some way to bring up the subject of money again. I've been living on cold beans and slices. My dad neatly wipes his mouth with a napkin, and then I know I'm dumb. The cheese in my mouth burns the roof. My dad starts to get up to go, saying Well and Alrighty and I Guess So and Anyways.

I pat him on the butt and say not to worry about me, that I'll just go down to the corner and beg. And then it comes: Are you sure you don't want any money? Okay, and whatever, I could be persuaded to take a few small bills, nothing too big of course.

How much do you want?

Be careful now, Mina, be careful, not too much. But why not get what you can? I roll my eyes and do the math and go, maybe two hundred? It's a little more than he was expecting, but he drops his head and nods. From his back pocket he pulls out a beige wallet that smells like new leather and counts out two hundred dollar bills.

I take them without talking and whatever. He's all embarrassed and goes, They're new because I just went to the bank before I came here. I shake my head. He tries to hold me for a second but I slip away before things get ridiculous. I should be crying. Then he leaves and says, You know where I live. I go out onto Telegraph. I should be crying. Broken glass is in the street, but no people, and I can't breathe. My father the grown man has given two hundred bucks to a stranger. I want to buy something. There's nothing good to buy. When I get bored I think I'll become a lesbian and move to Guyana.

Talisman

from the novel *Lawnboy*

by Paul Lisicky

AT THIRTEEN, I WAS AFRAID OF A CERTAIN KIND OF FAG.
I did everything possible to distinguish myself from him. I
recorded my voice over and over, imagining hard flat stones on
my tongue, working out the inflections, sanding over any last
traces of hiss or sibilance. I trudged back and forth down the
length of our driveway, taking heavy, self-assured steps, bouncing
just slightly from the knees until my arms swung naturally, without concentration. I did pushups by the dozen on the laundry
room floor. I read sports page after sports page, memorizing the
scores, insinuating myself into arguments in which the merit of
the Marlins' MVP was in question. There was nothing weak
about me. You could say that I talked too much, that I was scattered and lacked the ability to concentrate, that I hungered for
overwhelming amounts of attention and reassurance from
everyone who came into contact with me, but you wouldn't
have said that I was feminine—of that much I was sure.

Unlike Stan Laskin. Stan Laskin: hardware store owner. Stan
Laskin: who paid special attention to me every time I was sent in
by Sid, my father, to buy switches or ten-penny nails. It wasn't
that he was kind to me. It was that his body, his entire self-pre-
sentation, soft and yielding, with its tendency toward flab, represented everything that made me fearful of myself. His
colognes perfumed the atmosphere every time I waited at his
counter. His glasses, which changed daily depending upon his

outfit, coordinated with his bracelets and rings. But most dis-
turbing of all was the expression on his face, wounded and doe-
like, even pretty, as if he were waiting for some devastating
stranger to come striding in through the door.

As far as I knew he lived alone and had never been loved by
anyone in his life. His days, I imagined, were repetitive, dull,
and constrained, enlivened only by occasional visits to the fabric
store, where he remembered all the employees' birthdays, and to
the public bathroom stall where he sat six hours at a time before
a vacant glory hole. After work, I pictured him walking through
his front door, leaving his outer life behind and assuming a
secret role without any constraints, draping himself in chiffon
or chintz, before giving hairdos to his Yorkshires or trying on
his extensive collection of cloches, pins, and costume jewelry.
Every couple of days he'd call up his mother, and talk to her for a
full two hours, discussing the trip they were planning to the
Italian Alps. His life had as much to do with my own as an issue
of *McCall's*.

It was a warm, dark day in December, the second weekend
before Christmas. A heat wave was descending upon Dade
County, moistening the foliage with dew. In Florida fashion, the
trunks of the palms were wrapped with strings of clear lights. I
was hurrying down the Miracle Mile with Mark Margolit and
Steve Mendelsohn, two of my friends from school. At least I
thought they were friends. I cared about them as much as I cared
about the health of my gums, but to each other we looked like
friends, and when the three of us were together no one dared
make fun of us. I felt convincing with them. They entirely
believed me when I expressed my interest in my friend, Jane.
Together, we talked about the color and texture of Jamaica
Reed's nipples, the lead guitar solos from Metallica's second
album, and the afterschool activities of Mrs. Walgreen, our

Spanish teacher, who was forever tugging her miniskirt down over her hip. I wore a ripped Ozzy Osborne t-shirt with black kohl eyeliner around my eyes, and when I looked in the mirror I even scared myself.

We walked around the perimeter of the circle, the scent of frozen pizza still rising from our fingers, stumbling to the video arcade, where we'd play a few games of Donkey Kong or Burger Time. In my thirteen year old way, I'd told myself I was having fun and was behaving like any boy my age was supposed to. We couldn't have been walking more than ten seconds when I saw Stan Laskin carrying boxes between a rent-a-truck and his store, accepting a delivery. He looked relatively normal for Stan Laskin: loose chino pants, striped button–down. Except for the piece of material—an intricate brocaded print, tied around his throat like an ascot. My stomach lurched. I felt nothing but embarrassed and afraid for him.

"Nice scarf," Steve muttered.

He didn't look at us. He hefted up a box marked screwdrivers, almost dropping it in the process.

"Butterfingers," Steve said. "Do you always walk around wearing women's clothes?"

It got him that time. His face went crimson, grimacing. I stood silently beside Steve, my arms drawn tight to my sides, offering neither support nor discouragement.

"For your information it's an ascot," Stan Laskin mumbled.

"Oh, an ascot," Steve said, mocking his voice. "An *ass* —cot. How nice."

"Let's get out of here," I said to Mike.

"No way." Steve's whole being surged, unsettled, excited by his daring. He leapt up toward the stop sign and slapped at its red metal face.

"Do you like to suck cock?"

No response.

"Do you? Do you like the taste of cock in your mouth?"

Still, no response.

"Faggot," Steve said, in full earshot of Stan's customers. "Fucking, repulsive, cocksucking faggot."

I was practically shaking now. It was time to move on. I hoped that Stan would ignore it all, understanding where this was coming from. Instead, he stopped, then turned not to Steve, but to me. He looked into my face in a harder, more searching way than anybody had ever done.

"What made you so hateful?" he said.

I looked back at him, speechless.

"You of all people. I thought you were decent."

I stared down at the stained pavement, face burning red. I couldn't begin to explain.

"Fuck you," Steve said. "Come on, Sarshik. Come on, Margolit. Let's get the hell out of here."

I thought about the incident for days. I completed my activities as usual: I tossed Milk Duds to Delaware, our Boston terrier, in my efforts to teach her how to fetch. I worked through all the supplementary exercises in my algebra packet, achieving a 98 on the pop quiz. I even helped Peter, my brother, wax my father's Grand Prix, buffing its blue finish with a chamois cloth, something I'd never done before. At night, though, lying in bed, I couldn't push the image of Stan Laskin's face from my thoughts. I tried to tell myself that what had happened hadn't been so wretched. Everyone behaved that way, everyone I knew. It wasn't like they meant any harm. It was the way you carried yourself in the world. Otherwise, you'd be pounded down yourself. Faggot, cocksucker, queer: these were just words—empty, stupid, meaningless words. No one needed to be defended here.

What the hell was I so afraid of?

I was standing in the locker room after gym class. We were midway through the swimming unit, which I preferred to softball or to flag football. Nearly everyone had already left for homeroom. The air smelled of unwashed socks. I looked from side to side, pulled down my gym shorts, a little shy, before I heard the pounding spray of the shower room. I glanced over my shoulder. It was Jon Brainard, a small, intense boy with dark eyes and hair, who'd transferred the month before from Sarasota. He kept looking at me. Beneath the showerhead, his body looked luminous and silvered, hard defined hands lathering a compact chest. He might have been my brother in another time. My fingers tingled and chilled. He was rinsing the suds from his upper legs. I couldn't keep myself from staring, though I wanted to stop it.

"Evan Sarshik," he called.

I looked away. I wouldn't answer.

"Afraid to take a shower?"

The drain gulped down the overflow. The smile on his face was smug, as if he knew something about me I hadn't imagined.

I might have run through the door.

Many months passed before I again permitted myself to walk into Stan Laskin's Tru-Value. It smelled of sawdust, wet matches, mouse droppings, mothballs—a heady cocktail of fragrances which I associate, to this day, only with that place. In my pocket, I carried an arrowhead, something which I'd found behind a croton on the Metrozoo grounds. It was my talisman, my lucky charm. I had attributed several minor miracles to its existence, among them the recovery of a lost fifty dollar bill and the rapid healing of my sprained ankle. My plan was this: to leave it on his counter in an unmarked bag without note or explanation. He could do with it what he wanted. I knew it was unreasonable, and I knew it was inane, but the exchange had been hovering over me for weeks, a black nebulous carpet, and I just wanted to get things off my mind.

Stan Laskin was nowhere in sight. I positioned the lunch bag against the cash register, then turned toward the door to make a quick getaway.

At once he came toward me with crowbar in hand. He looked blankly at me, as if he thought I needed help. All at once his face winced, contorted.

"I know you."

My heart slowed. I imagined him bringing the crowbar down once across my forehead, splitting it in two.

"You were one of those boys," he said. "Get out of here."

"But—"

"You get the fucking hell out of here."

I walked out of the store without explaining myself. It was the voice and not the crowbar that frightened me. Even then, I knew that it wasn't just about my cruelty and indifference, but every time he'd heard the word *faggot* muttered behind his back. That night, lying on the living room sofa, I thought about the arrowhead in the lunch bag. It was a stupid, meaningless gesture that meant absolutely nothing to him, I'm positive. I'm sure he even tossed it in the trash. But there was always the chance that he kept it, and it's serving him now, giving him luck, warding off anyone who'd try to hurl a word at him.

Animals And The Zoo

by Denise Duhamel

I STARTED MY PERIOD THE DAY BEFORE SEVENTH
grade, which in most American towns is the first grade in junior
high. Woonsocket's junior high was so bad it was called The
Zoo—kids getting pushed into the Blackstone River which was
polluted by textile mills, pregnant girls smoking brown More
cigarettes, boys with after-shave that smelled like laundry
detergent. I tried to wear the right thing which I thought was a
red mini-skirt with a red blazer except since my mother sewed
most of our clothes and she'd run out of material this blazer had
short puffy sleeves. I wore saddle shoes, except it was the seventies so these particular ones had platform soles made of red
sponge. My pantyhose were a dark shade because I thought this
way my legs would look tanned—they were a shiny brand on
the advice of my best friend who said such a style made our legs
look thinner. Sanitary pads then were held up by belts and Moddess had strips of paper in the front and back that had to be
worked elaborately into the metal belt hooks, not unlike tight-
ening the straps on your back pack or those that lead to the bib
of your overalls. I was kind of a skinny thirteen year old since I
ate only half of everything on my plate ever since I started getting breasts so those Moddess seemed huge under my skirt and I
was sure everyone knew I was menstruating. I went to the bathroom between every class and was careful not to squirm in my
seat because who knew which way that sanitary napkin could
slide, riding up my back or up towards my belly. I don't remem-

ber if I had pubic hair yet, or how much. I never saw any of it grow in—I didn't look down until I was sixteen and even then I was surprised and a little scared about what was there. Samuel Jackson, the actor who became famous for his outlaw/born-again ways in *Pulp Fiction*, said once when the kids in his neighborhood were playing war, he went into the bathroom to find his mother's napkins and tied one with those by-gone strips around his head to show he was play-wounded. Of course, he had no idea what the napkins were really for, he tells Jay Leno and the audience laughs. My sister didn't know either since she was a year younger and I was amazed that we would go into public toilets at the movies or in restaurants and she would walk right by that white metal machine with the rusted corners that was stuck to the wall like a medicine cabinet, that she wouldn't notice that woman with the blond swept-up hair smelling daisies, who was serenely menstruating, taking the week off to spend in a field. My mother complained that I went through too many pads, that I should wait a few hours before changing them. She held up the baby blue box and said *I can't afford to have you go through one of these a day.* I didn't like the squish between my legs and feared gushes like urine when I least expected them. It took me a long time to trust my mother who promised that wouldn't happen, to find my rhythm, that first two days heavy, the third day the cramps, the fourth day nearly gone, the blood coming back one more day on the fifth. My grandmother had to use strips of cotton cloth then wash them in cold water, chapping her hands, her mother dying before her period came so that when she had her first she ran into the barn screaming, sure she was dying too and refused to tell her father what was wrong. She said she sat there with the animals, a horse she usually took care of licking her cheeks. She held onto a lamb, she petted the sheep until her father figured out what was happening, but had no idea what to say. He called upon an aunt who snipped the corners of an old bed sheet then tore it into squares my grandmother could fold and pin into the crotch of her bloomers. *You girls have it so lucky these days,* she told me, rather shyly, just before she died, just before the first tampon TV commercials, just before the lucky pairing of sanitary napkins and adhesive.

Dogwood

from the novel *The World According to My Tongue*

by Chester Freeman

DADDY'S RIGHT EYE TURNED RED IN THE CORNER, a staph infection. At St. Luke's they shaved his head and cut him ear to ear, like slicing a watermelon, and still couldn't get all the infection out. Daddy would unwrap his bandage and show off the Jack-o-lantern grin to my school friends. His bald head was the color of chalk. I told him his scar would do Frankenstein proud. "*Master*," he growled and raised his arms like a couple of hairy two-by-fours. His eyes already looked the part, sleepy. I tasted the clear stuff the doctor gave Mom to put in Daddy's eye.

Back home Daddy read westerns and sheet music with his good eye, and practiced the trombone until his headaches got too bad. His fever wouldn't go away, and Mom and me brought him back to the hospital.

I counted floor tiles, followed the nurses around, looked for things to taste. An intern taught me chess.

Later on, Daddy talked in his sleep. He talked to his father, who's buried way up north in New Jersey, and his dead father talked back. Then he asked who Rennie was. He thought me and Jewel were his only children. Rennie was just starting to talk. Then, something about corpuscles, Mom said. It got into his blood, Doctor Grimes said. Doctor Grimes combed his grey hair same as Daddy, back and pushed up from his ears, like wings, with little waves on top. Daddy's was black as a fresh-tarred road.

At Daddy's funeral I peeled a white petal from a rose and kept it under my tongue till it crumbled.

After, I had to get into bed with Mom some nights. She cried, it was Niagara Falls for a while. Almost four years ago, I was seven. Daddy died from blood poisoning my third week of school, during recess while I was losing to Harold Mott's big brother at chess and for once not thinking about him.

From the interstate I see a red glow over the mountains. I say it's a fire. Mom glances out my window, squints and says it's the sun setting. Once the sun's gone and Mom has steered the Chevy off the interstate and onto an old blacktop highway, I can't see a thing for the trees.

Mom stares out my window. A shadow sweeps over her face, and she gets such a look. It's like this shadow has a voice and whispered some secret to her on its way. I want to put my fingers on her face, like how blind people do. When we pass a wooden sign on my side, best something-or-other in Alabama, I tell Mom we're in Alabama now. She doesn't even nod.

I ask her, "What're ya thinking?"

"I'm looking for something." She glances in the back seat, then looks down at me and smiles, and shakes her head. "It's a surprise."

Rennie's already asleep on the back seat with her knees under her chin and her dirty hair in her mouth. She's scribbled all over the back of her hand with an ink pen. Jewel's facing her, her freckled legs crossed, counting out 50s and 100s and 500s of the raggedy Monopoly bills Rennie always takes on long car trips, and won't let anyone touch usually. Jewel's only nine, but can talk a bear out of a honey comb and then convince it to go find her a spoon.

Mom turns left off the highway onto a dark spooky road she says is a shortcut through the mountains to 281.

Ben's waiting on us in Georgia.

Jewel leans over the seat and says for the umpteenth time, "I'm bored."

I find a dog-eared booklet of word puzzles in the glove compartment and toss it into the back seat. "Knock yerself out," I tell her.

All Mom's talked about the last hour is Ben, her latest beau. How Ben grew up on a farm in Mississippi, poor, youngest of nine, his mother and father too old and worn out to be a mother and father by the time he needed them, how he was raised by his sisters, who spoiled him. Ben didn't even finish high school.

"Imagine, Lloyd, being spoiled and poor," Mom keeps saying.

She talks like all this Ben stuff is just to pass the time. But she's sly, she's capturing all my pawns *en passant*, building up to something, and I know what. Mom wants to get married again.

81 across Alabama, then north to Rome. Ben's welding pipe seams and flanges at a chemical plant, two going on three months now, working off his union card. Nobody at his hall's supposed to know he's there, he would lose his card for Arkansas. He's cheating, in other words. We're supposed to have a chess match, Ben and I, only he keeps putting it off. Probably because you can't cheat at chess.

I made up my own variation of the French defense. I can think twelve moves ahead, foresee just about anything that might happen. It's like knowing the Indian trails that wind through the five mountains that surround Hot Springs, where the Dogwood Trail cuts off and joins the trail that leads to Reserve Street, how many ways there are of getting from Hot Springs Mountain to North Mountain, or to the camp site, and how many ways there are of getting out of the mountains and where you'll end up, in town or outside of it.

Ben tried to be dapper the first day he came to see Mom, wearing a sport coat he couldn't button at his belly over a wrinkled shirt, and shiny black shoes that squeaked. Me and Mom had a good laugh. White trash, or pretty close to it. This was eight months ago. I felt sorry for Ben after Mom left the daffodils he'd brought her laying on the kitchen table. He'd told some story about his mother wanting nothing but daffodils at her funeral, and how sad it was when there was hardly any at her funeral. Then one day Ben brought a book of poems, 101 Love Poems or something, and even read a poem about daffodils out loud, hick accent and all. It had to have been the sappiest poem in the book, I wouldn't repeat it to a dead dog. But Mom stopped making fun of Ben after that, just when it was getting good.

The trees crowd up close to the hilly road, the high beams bounce off low-hanging branches, and it seems like we're sliding down through a tunnel of leaves.

I want to tell Mom how pretty she is, too pretty for Ben.

"Silly," she calls me, when she catches me staring at her.

"What would you say to spending these last three weeks of the summer in Georgia?" Mom asks me. "With Ben?"

"Might be more fun than bumming around Hot Springs while all the other kids are at camp. "

Hot Springs, Arkansas, that's were we live, where Mom grew up. And summer camp's one of the things we can't afford anymore.

"Camp's near about over," I say.

"Three whole weeks without your sisters. Think you can stand that?"

"You and me and Ben?"

"You and Ben," she says. "Ben likes the idea. The men work in shifts, and fish a lot. That is all they do, the way I hear it."

Daddy used to take me to the lakes near the college. Mom thinks I like fishing. I hated fishing even then, I just liked watching the students in their sail boats, and the ducks and being with Daddy.

Mom pats my leg and says, "Think about it. There's plenty of time."

Mom gets cheery. Maybe I should get cheery too, but I don't feel cheery. I feel like a crumpled-up piece of paper someone made a mistake on.

"Did I tell you Ben's taking us to the park?" she asks. "Have you and I ever been to the Chatahoochee Park before?"

"Chata*who*?" I ask, and pull a piece of foam stuffing from a crack in the seat to chew on.

Still cheery, she says, "Hoochee, as in hoochee-koochee," letting my shitty question slide. "I'm planning a picnic. So think about what you'll he hungry for. Got a craving?"

But now Mom's easing up on the gas again, twisting her palms hard on the wheel, glancing out her window. She stops in the middle of the road and looks through a clearing, across a weedy ditch, then backs the Chevy to an old mailbox sitting cockeyed on a post between a crooked dirt driveway and an old Vote for George Wallace for Governor sign.

I do have a craving. I can't think what it is.

Mom whispers, "This is the house, Lloyd. Can you believe?"

I can hardly see the house for all the weeds, and the dark.

Mom takes a Kleenex out of her purse and wads it once around her finger, but doesn't use it. False alarm. I want to hug her but force myself not to.

Mom cuts the lights, leans over the wheel and sets her chin on her bony knuckles. I can see where she shaved her underarms too close.

She clears her throat, says to me, still gawking at the house, "Guess who spent the night here once?" She raises her eyebrows at me. "'Your daddy. The two of us."

Just the way she says it, *your daddy*...

"When?" I ask.

"Long time ago. It wasn't so run down then. We got stranded on our way to a Dixieland gig outside Atlanta," Mom says. She looks into the back seat where both Rennie and Jewel are asleep, then digs like a squirrel into her Pall Malls. "You remember that old Rambler?"

"The jolly green dragon," I remind her.

"It started raining," Mom's saying. "Hard. When it didn't look like anybody was coming home, or the rain let up…"

"Where was I?"

Mom takes her pinky nail from between her teeth, puffs on her cig and says, "Where indeed," smiling like she's got a secret. "Guess what happened right there in that window where the light's on, ten years ago, plus…oh, eleven months give or take?"

I add up the months, then feel like I've been smacked in the face.

Mom gives my neck a squeeze and says, "I was pretty wild then. Daddy, too. Need a hint?"

"No thanks."

"*You* happened, silly," Mom says. "You were conceived."

She's holding my hand now.

"I know it was then because I went almost three weeks without seeing your daddy, and when he got home we hit the road again, and ended up stuck out here…"

"I git it," I say, and snatch my hand back. "Can we just git going?"

Mom mashes her cig out in the tray and turns the motor off, grabs my hand again, and says, "Come on."

"Come on where?"

"I'm curious. It won't hurt you, not too much."

And when I tug back and squint at her, and whisper, "Yer gonna tell them you and Daddy did it in their house," she rolls her eyes in a big way and says, "With a bit more tact than that, though. They might get a laugh out of it. And so what if they don't? What's the worst that can happen?"

Her favorite question.

But she doesn't really think ahead. In chess you have to think ahead, and in lots of different directions. A king's pawn opening means one thing, a queen's pawn another, a knight opening something else. What if this, and what if that.

"They could shoot us in the butt with rock salt," I say.

She bites her bottom lip and stares at the house like there's a prize waiting for her inside. Before I can think of the next what-if, she opens her door and says, "I'll go by myself then. Just as well. You can babysit your sisters."

The next what-if comes to me, and I ask her about Ben, who's waiting on us right across the state line. Who'll be worried about us taking so long. "Ain't my fault I got conceived out here in the boonies," I say.

She picks up her purse and then changes her mind and sets the purse back on the seat. Then she whispers, "Ben's not exactly waiting on us. We're surprising him."

Rennie's awake and calling out the back window. "Can I go too?"

Mom motions with her hand and Rennie scoots out the Chevy and dashes through the weeds.

On the porch Mom uses her Kleenex to wipe off the sides of her shoes. I watch from the car.

"You're on yer own," I whisper, and pull at the crack in the seat till my hand is full of the brown foam. I toss the foam on the floor and slip out of my pocket the sketches I drew yesterday. I traced a woman from a Yellow Pages ad. I can draw most anything except faces, but chess is what I'm best at.

Staring at the bed sheet hung over the windows of the house, something ugly crosses my mind, in and out, like a buzzard circling over a dead armadillo.

Jewel pops her face over the seat and says, being the smartass she is, "So...This is where it all started for you." She'd been pretending to be asleep the whole time. "Lloyd Delaney, this is your life."

"Ha ha," I say. "You should team up with Edgar Bergen."

I climb out of the Chevy, jump mud holes and pee in the weeds, listening to the crickets chirp. They sound like a zillion marbles rattling in a sack.

Jewel hollers from the Chevy, "Go tell Mom to come on."

I get just close enough to the house to hear a piano going, way out of tune, and I can tell it's Mom playing it. She used to play piano with Daddy's jazz band. The house close-up looks tacked together with spit, like dirt daubers built it.

The porch creeks under me feet. I look through a window, past the stained bed sheet. An old woman and a little girl holding a prissy-looking doll under her arm are sitting on a ratty sofa. White trash, suffice to say. And there's Mom playing the piano, plunking away like she doesn't care how out of tune it is. Her wrists flick and her fingers hop off the keys. I wonder if she's pretending to be happy, like she's been doing since Daddy died, or if she really is happy.

Back on the spooky road, Mom gets us lost. The map's no help. Instead of doubling back, Mom just keeps driving, hoping we'll come out somewhere, like the interstate will find us. She really thinks this way. But I know things don't work like that. You move and move, and hope for the best, you end up checkmated.

"We're heading the right way," she keeps saying.

"What's that smell?" Jewel asks.

The road gets hilly. We pass an empty police car parked on the side of the road, some striped sawhorses and orange barrels laying on their sides.

"I don't think we oughta be on this road," I tell Mom.

Jewel says, "Somebody's roasting weenies, I think."

At the top of a hill the trees clear on our right. Mom stops in the middle of the road, and Jewel wakes Rennie. All of us stare out the windows. I knew it wasn't the sun. The flames stretch in all directions but ours, and for as far into the night as we can see. The sky could be falling, looks like.

"Look," Jewel says, pointing to where a bunch of little houses are burning.

Mom turns the Chevy around.

"Those folks need to get out of there," Mom says, of the people with the George Wallace sign in their yard.

But now she can't find the house again. She's made another wrong turn, and after thirty minutes of driving around in circles, we end up back at the interstate, which is what she'd been looking for in the first place.

The Chevy growls up the ramp, heading east.

After a while Mom whispers to herself, "They'll find their way out, I'm sure."

The rest of the way to Georgia, no one says a word. Mom takes out a Kleenex and this time uses it.

They sit outside in the dark by the pool, Mom and Ben, on two wet Motel 8 lounge chairs, talking. We sure surprised Ben, alright. He's still surprised, I can see it in his face even from here. If I were a deaf person, I could read their lips, too. "We won't be long," Mom told us. That was over an hour ago. I watch from the motel room window, and I'm thinking I'll go out and sit at the table next to Mom anyway, just so they'll stop talking. Grown-ups can talk themselves into any stupid thing. They could stand up and shake hands and go their separate ways, which would suit me fine, or they could walk in here arm in arm and make some lame announcement.

While Jewel's in the bathroom and Rennie's not paying attention, I go through the pockets of Ben's windbreaker and work pants, which he left on a chair in our room. A heavy key chain with a monkey made from a peach seed, a pocket knife, change, lint, two dollar bills, and a crumpled bar napkin with a phone number written on it—written with an eye liner pencil. It's either that or an artist's pastel. I've got a bunch back home I never use.

When I look again, Mom and Ben are just sitting quietly, thinking and smoking, not even looking at each other. And now I can't decide which is worse, talking to each other or thinking to themselves. Finally, Ben scoots his chair next to Mom. When she lets him kiss the inside of her hand, I close the curtains.

Ben comes straight to our room after work looking like a wounded soldier, with his welding hood hung under his arm, and a double ring of dirt across his forehead. Only he's no soldier. He looks as awkward as a welder as he did eight months ago as a suitor. We pile into the Chevy, Ben behind the wheel, and head for the Chattahoochee Forest. Mom searches the car's radio for more news of the fire. We can't find out if the fire's still burning or not. Ben's already warning Mom we might get rained on. The sky's been dull all morning with dark big-bellied clouds. One good long rain would take care of the forest fire, Mom says. There's a sharp edge to Mom's voice.

Mom spreads the map on her knees and checks directions after Ben turns off the highway onto a narrow road. Just like Mom two days ago, Ben says he knows where he's going.

"Not another short-cut," Jewel says. "Let me outa here."

Mom's already told Ben about the house in the woods, playing the out-of-tune piano, getting lost. Everything except why we stopped in the first place. She told Ben we were just stopping for directions, then she winked at me.

I slip the bar napkin from my back pocket and read the phone number on it. But I stare at the numbers too long. Maybe it isn't even a phone number.

Jewel leans her elbows on the seat next to Mom and says, "I got a question. Hey Ben..." and Mom butts in before she can finish.

"*Mister* Ben," Mom says.

"Mister... How long is a rope?" Jewel asks.

Ben glances in the rearview. Then he smiles at Mom and says, "I give. How long's a rope?"

Jewel slaps her palm on the back of the seat. "Twice half its length," she says, then laughs and flops back down between me and Rennie.

Ben laughs.

"I got another," Jewel says. "How far can you walk into the woods?"

Ben shrugs.

"Halfway. Any further and you'll be walking *out* of the woods."

"Clever gal," Ben says.

"Don't encourage her, " Mom tells him.

The downpour starts, like God above tripped and accidentally spilled it.

"Looks like a toad-strangler," Ben says, and pulls off the road.

The map fills up the car with an annoying racket when Mom tries to fold it back the way it was. Mom throws up her hands. Everyone gets quiet, even Ben. He lights a cig and breathes the smoke against the windshield. We wait at a gas station for the traffic to loosen up.

Then the rain turns to drizzle all of a sudden and then stops as quick as it started.

Mom says, "Let's give it a try, at least. We're so close."

There's a skimpy waterfall, and Mom says to stop. We park under a tree and roll down all the windows because Ben says things might steam up again.

"Awful hot for November," Ben says, then looks at Mom. "The rain could cool things off a mite."

Mom spreads the boiled eggs and noodle salad and loaf of bread, a can of caviar, potato chips and corn chips, and plastic forks and knives on the blanket.

Jewel holds the can of caviar to her nose and makes a face. "Must be jelly 'cause jam don't shake like dat," she says, to break the silence.

I dip a Saltine into the shiny orange eggs and eat it whole.

"You like that stuff?" Ben asks me. "Me and Miss Jewel'll stick with the fish," he says.

He reaches over and tweaks Jewel on the cheek, and I wait for Jewel to say something snotty, at least give him her I'd-like-to-watch-you-die look. Her face goes red instead.

"Okay, Mister and Missus Hick," I say to Ben and Jewel.

Mom looks up from her chips. "Apologize."

"Sorry," I say quickly, not looking at Ben.

"What about you, squirt?" Ben asks Rennie. "You sensible, or highfalutin?"

Rennie eats a little caviar off the end of her finger and grins at Mom.

"Don't jump to any conclusions,'" Jewel says. "She...she..." But Jewel gets tongue-tied. "She eats mud if you don't watch her," Jewel finally says.

Everybody laughs at Jewel, even Jewel.

I walk up to the Chevy, where Mom's sitting in the middle of the seat and listening to the radio, and staring out the windshield at nothing. Sunlight keeps winking on and off. Mom notices me after I clear my throat.

"Nothing about the fire," she tells me.

I think she's about to say something else to me, something important, maybe even some secret. But Ben walks up.

"What say we walk back down to that waterfall?" Ben asks.

Mom stretches her arms behind her head and yawns. "I could use a walk."

We follow Mom and Ben down the narrow road. Ben rattles his keys in his pocket.

"Not too much further," Ben says, and takes a hold of Mom's elbow.

The closer to the waterfall you get, the more pennies and nickels and dimes and quarters you can see at the bottom with the sun bouncing off them. Jewel and Rennie go ape, scooping up all the wet change they can stuff into their pockets. "It ain't stealing," Jewel whispers to Rennie.

"That's bad luck," Mom says.

"*Good* luck, you mean," Jewel says. She's plucking coins out of the water like crazy.

"Those are people's wishes you're sticking in your pockets."

Mom gets annoyed with them, and makes Jewel and Rennie empty their pockets and leave the coins where they found them.

"It's stealing," Mom says.

"It's finding," Jewel says back.

I wade over to the fall and stick my hand through the sheet of water that's sliding between the rocks and hitting at my feet. It's warmer than the water I'm standing in for some reason, and noisy. I hold my hands together under the waterfall, like I'm praying, then open them at the palms and part the water just enough to see the green stones piled together, slimed-over and fuzzy in the cracks, but some smooth and shiny as Mom's best china. I touch the smooth stones. My fingers stink from touching the slimy ones. I taste the slime from my fingers.

When I look again, Jewel and Rennie are squatting on the bank counting out pebbles they've collected in place of the coins. Mom's still barefoot in the stream but looking up at the mountain that looks down on us. I can't tell what mood she's in. When I spy Ben on the bank, standing there with Mom's shoes in one hand and her socks in the other, he looks the most awkward I've seen him. His black shiny shoes are out of place on the side of the stream.

On the bank I realize how wet my pants are. I pull my sketches from my pocket but I'm too late, they're soaked, stuck together. The number on the bar napkin is washed away. I wad the wet napkin up and slip it into my mouth.

At one corner of the clearing, far from the stream, I find a dirt trail. Just like the Indian trails in the mountains back home. The wide mouth of the trail calls to me. The woods are quiet, though. I can't even hear a bird chirping, just the few dead leaves under my feet as I cut off onto a trail that smells of dogwood. The trails are narrow and dusty. Rain couldn't get to parts of the trail for all the leaves overhead. A squirrel dashes up a tree. I watch for Indians.

It comes to me, this isn't the Dogwood Trail. I'm going from trail to trail like I know them. I head back, and at the first split I don't know which way to go. I am not lost, I tell myself. Jewel will never let me live this down. I turn left and keep walking, but nothing looks familiar. A lizard skitters through the leaves just off the trail. The ground crackles. The trail dips, I don't remember walking uphill this far. In the distance, through the trees I see brick houses, yards and barbecue pits, cars. I head back, take the other trail. I'm running before I realize it. At another fork I stop and holler, then holler again, louder, holler for Daddy. My voice echoes. It doesn't sound like me. It sounds like some white trash kid. I have an accent. I start running, not thinking, just running, and whispering to God how I'll give up everything, even chess, and take back every mean thing I said and thought about Ben, about everybody.

Then I'm back at the stream, only farther up. Rennie and Jewel are on the bank. Ben's gone. Mom is still in the stream. Her clothes are wet, she must have slipped. She looks up and waves to me, and smiles, and I wave back like nothing has happened, like my heart is not pushing up into my throat. Like it isn't still running through the woods.

Half Acre Crawl

by Christine Liotta

I DIVE INTO THE BRIGHT BLUE SWIMMING POOL SET DEEP in our back yard; the water, a rectangle of brilliant color against the green lawn. Under water, the sound of our dog Max's barking sounds distant and muffled, as if he were suddenly very far away. He jumps into the pool after me and I swim away from him in my best crawl stroke, afraid he is a man trapped in a dog's body. Maybe he understands everything I say. When I turn my head for breath, I see my parents on the wood deck, preparing for the party this evening. Father is unfolding yellow and green plastic lawn chairs and arranging them in neat half circles. Mother is wearing her black wraparound skirt with turquoise butterflies. She is sticking colored toothpicks into cheese cubes. Next, Mother and Father have their arms around each others' waists, and I am standing in front of them. My father's hand rests on the shoulder strap of my bathing suit when the picture is taken. I am helping with the cheese cubes and bayberry scented candles and plastic champagne glasses. At the side of the house, our dog Max slips out through a gap in the fence and starts to run away. I pretend not to notice and continue slicing the pepperoni, but my father notices and yells at me to go after the dog. His voice is like thunder; his silver sunglasses reflect my small pale face back at me. I will do as I am told. One day I hide behind Father's big chair in the living room all day. My parents think I am lost. I hear them call the police and describe what I look like, what bathing suit I am wearing. I hear Mother crying. One early summer evening the sun casts an orange glow over the pool and hangs low in the sky behind our yard. My boyfriend is swimming with me; he is swimming after me and I am swimming away from him, but he catches up with me in the deep end. The golden hairs on his tanned forearms and chest catch the light, and he kisses me wetly. I tell him that I am never getting married. He doesn't say anything, but slides the straps of my bathing suit down over my freckled shoulders before we make love. Our entwined limbs seem horribly distorted under the surface of the water, as if they had all been broken and then braided together. My mother tells me that I should date other boys; that I've made it too easy for him. She tells me a cliché, about buying a cow and about getting milk for free. I think: What if I like to drink milk, too? I think: What if I like to drink chocolate milk? One week and six days later, my boyfriend leaves for college to become a dermatologist. Three weeks later he forgets to call me on my birthday. All through one hot slow summer, the lover I am waiting for is far away. I dream that he has tried to drown me. I try to plant a vegetable garden, get a job, and forget his dark hair and full lips. I get a job in the paleontology department at the museum sorting fossils, bone fragments, and vertebrae into plastic trays with multiple compartments, but quit after two weeks. At home, I turn the fresh earth where my garden will be over and over with a shovel. My parents are worried about me; they encourage other interests. I try to forget.

We are at the beach. Father is pushing me through the gentle waves, calling me his little fish. We are laughing. As I come up for air, I see Mother on the sand in a low canvas chair with red stripes. She is wearing a straw hat and sunglasses. She looks angry. I call to her that I am a fish, then she smiles and waves her white hands at me. I swim faster, doing laps from one end of our pool to the other while the party goes on around me. Mother tries to coax me out of the water. From the pool, I have a clear view of hairy ankles bulging over dark loafers, or pink and orange toenails peeking out from white strapless sandals. Tonight, the pool area is illuminated by a spotlight, several candles, and the occasional flash of a camera. Three soggy potato chips float by as I hang beneath the diving board, watching. I climb the white plastic steps, wrap myself in a towel, and join my parents at the buffet table, which is covered with round cheeses and colorful bowls of fruits and fondues and dips. "You're such a darling," says Mrs. Wagner, touching my shoulder with one hand as she pops a slice of kiwi into her red mouth with her other. My inability to speak with my parents' friends, even after being directly spoken to, is alarming. It is as if my mouth would have to be pried open. My mother glares at me, gulps her wine. "Yes, wasn't it nice of my daughter to entertain us all." My father approaches with his arm around a young man. The young man wears a white sport jacket and navy tie. My father holds a plastic champagne glass filled with a sparkling liquid. They both smile as if their picture were being taken. I hear my father say: "Honey, this is Gerald Flynn. He's going to Princeton this fall." I tell him that I am going swimming and to drink his damn drink. I dive into the pool, smooth as an arrow. As I turn my head for breath, I can hear the voices of my parents, the neighbors, and the guests saying: "What? I don't know what you mean. What have you done with your hair?" On a wet night in July, I am in Atlantic City. The man with dark hair and full lips chases me in the rain and says that he loves me. I run as if I am running for my life while my white cotton pants become transparent from the rainwater. Two months later, I marry him in an informal ceremony at home. My mother makes her famous crab dip and artichoke pie. The summer after my father dies, my husband and I attend a party at a friend's beach house. I find myself alone on the sticky leather couch, with two flies circling above me, which remind me of my parents. I go outside for some air. There is my husband embracing another woman under the stairs. They are thin and tan and have curly hair. "Oh, hello," he says. According to the pattern we've established, he chases me, catches me, and tells me that it means nothing, that I am overreacting, that I'm too sensitive, that I must be drunk. My mother says she hates to say she told me so.

I am drifting, face down, before the guests arrive. I swim end to end without stopping until my arms begin to ache. My father sits in a green plastic lawn chair, reading a book that explains how to be your own nutritionist. Behind us, skydivers with their bright parachutes continue to drop from the sky like bombs, falling silently from the airplanes flying low in every direction. My father doesn't look up until Mr. Wagner arrives. My father greets Mr. Wagner with a drink in hand. I wade beneath the diving board. Three potato chips float by like desert islands. My mother tries to coax me out of the pool. Even Gerald Flynn leans over the edge of the pool as I swim by so that the tip of his navy tie gets wet. "What college do you want to go to?" he asks, and I kick water at him. On Sunday, a neighborhood boy with crooked teeth almost drowns while his parents are at a cocktail party at our house. When the police come, the whole party rushes across the street in their summer dresses and white cotton trousers and watch helplessly, breathlessly, as the boy receives mouth to mouth resuscitation on the open lawn. I watch from behind a peeling birch tree. The boy moves and everyone exhales. Before the child has stopped crying he has already forgotten what has happened to him. I feel as if I should have rescued the boy somehow. My father tells me to go home. I do as I am told. Later, the only other person to join me in the pool is Mrs. Wagner. In her black one-piece and matching bathing cap, she resembles a shiny wet olive. I watch from beneath the diving board as she inches into the pool, and the cold water creeps up her sturdy thighs, now covered with goose-flesh. All at once she flings herself into the pool with a great splash and a squeal. Weeks before my father dies, I marry. I swim faster than I did before. A friend tells me that she saw my husband with a woman with blonde hair. "They've been seen together a lot." I say: "Good for him." One hot slow summer I will plant a vegetable garden, look for a job, and try to forget. My main diet will consist of chocolate cake and mushrooms. I'll poke holes in the earth with my index finger for the basil seeds. I'll decide where to put the cucumbers and tomatoes and squash. In the evening, while I swim lap after lap, my arms and my sides begin to ache and I begin to have a very lifelike dream. It would be night time. My childhood bedroom would be drenched with stars and I would by lying in bed, looking at them, drawing relationships and shapes between them as if I were connecting the dots of a large star chart. My father would come in and sit on the edge of my bed and his shadow against the wall would look weary and hunched, like a tiger crushed underfoot by some mad elephant. He would look very tired and he would be there confessing something to me or apologizing or asking my advice. "It's tough," I would say. "It's just tough." Father is a good man. When he confesses in church he kneels in the dark booth for what seems like an eternity. What else could he be confessing except things that only he and I know? He isn't a heavy drinker. He doesn't even smoke. He works very hard at his job and comes back from the city every single night to be home with Mother and me. He feeds the dog. He buys us whatever we want. What else could such a man possibly have to confess; what else could weigh so heavily upon his conscience; what else could he possibly have to apologize for? "It's tough," I would say again. Then I'd see his eyes, dark blue. His eyes would cut me to slices, finally letting in the light. I'd swim into that famous blue. I wouldn't stop.

Anti-Autobiography

by William Pope.L

I

AS A CHILD I WAS OBSESSED WITH HEIGHTS. DURING summer vacations, I spent hours hanging upside down in the apple tree in our front yard. Looking down, I saw everything flattened out and contradictory. I saw the picket fence, directly below, come rushing up at me. Suddenly, my head ached and my knees were water. I tried calling for help but every time I opened my mouth, I wanted to vomit. My body was filled with a strange euphoria. I could smell my skin burning. I remained like so until darkness gathered in the branches...

Below me, the fence crouched in the darkness. Waiting to poke its white picket teeth in my little black body. I was late for dinner but no one had noticed I was missing. My voice hurt from yelling. No one had come calling. No one would come calling. Then just when I had almost given up hope, I was in my mother's arms and she was scolding me, beating me, scolding me while beating me with thin apple tree branches that cut into my arms and legs. Later, in bed, I touched my wounds and fell into a deep sleep. I dreamed I was an airplane made of skin, hollow and cold...

2

Now that I am an adult, I hate airplanes and anything to do with flying. To me, flying is not a symbol of freedom but of confinement, noise and bureaucracy. My favorite mode of travel is walking. This is a political statement not just whimsy ambulation. If I cannot walk, I take a car or a bus. So imagine my consternation at finding myself as I am now because…now…I am flying…

3

I am that jet fighter you see streaking across the horizon. But what you see is not what you get, my situation is far less glamorous, for I am not in a plane, I repeat, I am not in a plane, yet I am in the sky. You might ask, how can it be that I am in the sky, that I am flying yet have no jet, no plane in which to fly? How can this be? And I will answer: I was out walking. It was a saturday. I was in a good mood. Typical midsummer day. Ninety degrees in the shade, an ever so humble breeze stirring the air and a fat pompous sun in the sky.

I was headed for the Main St. Grocery at the corner of Cabinet and Main to buy a pack of cigarettes. I hadn't slept for days. My clothes stuck to my body. I was tired and giddy but my mind was incredibly clear. Before I left my apartment, I managed to put the finishing touches on the preface to my project. I have been working on this project ever since I can remember. In some sense, I am working on it right now in attempting to describe to you my present predicament. It was easier in the old days. The project was more innocent. At that time, it took the form of a liquid. I was trying to make a case for love. A traveling case. A traveling case for love. I discovered the perfect container was water. The problem was to keep it from evaporating…

4

On that hot saturday in question, for once, I didn't have my mind on the project. I walked through the glare, eyes half-closed, aware and not aware, barely side-stepping the broken green liquor bottles that littered the sidewalk...

Across the street, in front of the Park Ave. Laundromat, little black girls jumped rope and chanted double-dutch, their pig-tails defying gravity and the heat of the day. The asphalt glowed. Cars pulled up and sped away. The traffic lights changed from green to yellow to red...

5

I paused before an abandoned building. It was falling apart. Right before my eyes. I ran my hand across its shingles. A chalky shower of large green paint petals floated to the walk. The window was broken. I vaulted through and gashed my shoulder. I landed on the other side holding the wound, my feet sinking into something soft. Blood flowed down my arm, wet-ting my sleeve and filling my palm...

Inside the building, it was quiet, dim and cool. The air was damp and sweet. The room was tall and narrow like a hallway and from floor to ceiling the walls were lined with empty fish tanks and ani-mal cages. The ceiling was tin, very ornate, badly rusted and inhab-ited by hundreds of small birds that were swooping down upon a large mound in the middle of the room. The shape of their flight resembled a corkscrew and their flow never abated. Each bird, in its own turn, one after another, without pause, dived and spun, in an unbroken, ever-tightening spiral until an instant before impact, it veered off and disappeared back into a hole in the ceiling...

I approached the mound cupping my blood in my palm and plunged my hand into my curiosity and arrived where I am today. What I found in that mound, and how it led me, is not a secret, and I will divulge it briefly. But first, I will remind you that though this story comes in words, I am actually writing it with my presence. A presence riddled by my autobiography and my anti-autobiography. For I am not a man. I repeat, I am not a man. I am a black body streaking across the sky against the horizon. I have no cockpit to cover and protect me. I have no flight suit. No goggles. No pretty dials and knobs to make my incarceration rehabilitative. I have only my Adidas jogging suit, cut to ribbons by the wind. My shoulder throbs filled with glass. The ribbons of jogging suit whip my thighs and chest like metal saplings. I am...for lack of a better term...beyond me. My streak is cold and farcical. I have no address. The neighborhoods below do not touch me. Arrogance is my gasoline. Speed is my revise...I can smell my skin burning. I repeat, I can smell my skin burning. Whenever I smell my skin burning, I know my autobiography is getting the best of me. So I offer the worst of me to the rest of me, and of course, not far behind, I can hear the hooves of my anti-autobiography kicking up the difference between self and not-self...

Let me explain with a story, a story my Mum used to tell me after she beat me, a story about a woman she'd met in prison. My mother was there for dealing drugs. The woman was there for murder. Her story went like so: She and her husband were out for a night on the town, dressed in their finest togs. On a whim, they dropped by the neighborhood bar for a quick one. The lights in the bar were pretty. The couple felt festive and alive. The woman's blond wig sparkled astride her afro. Her husband's pink polyester evening jacket, with matching pants and vest, drew admiring stares from all present. They put quarters in the jukebox, danced, got smashed and began to argue. Over what, the woman would never recall. The next morning, she woke up in the gutter. Next to her, lay her husband. The witnesses said she'd killed him. The woman got 25 to life. We have alot in common that woman and me...

Like her, I am stuck in myself, against myself. For those of us between infinities, time is not the universal solvent. The woman will spend the rest of her life pacing her cell rubbing the skin off her face with her elbow, while I streak through the sky, past her window, leaving my autograph, in vapor trails, against the horizon...

6

Unlike 'Superman', I stand when I fly, always perpendicular to the horizon, I stand when I fly. This is not something I invented. It's not pretend. The seat of my pants is moist and weighty. I gave up on the simple amenities long ago. Indeed, I am not George Reeves. That was the name of the actor who played 'Superman' on television in the 50's and committed suicide by jumping off a building. He thought he could fly without the cameras. Though I sympathize with his end, I am completely indifferent to his means. Because in matters of fantasy, the end does not justify the means. It IS the means. Unavoidable. Everything, fact and datum. Fancy is just a pretty-fication of that which undoes us by its resistance to dissolution in the solution of our senses.

Fact: I am doing a job. Like a factory worker on the assembly-line of the celestial, I am chained to somebody else's idea of heaven. My streak, my streak, my streak is plain, unadorned, incontrovertible. Standing only increases my discomfort. Yet it is not my choice to stand. Had I a choice, I would sit. Or if walk I could, I'd stroll. Take in the sights. Pick wildflowers from the curbside and love everyone, every moment with every step I'd take, etc. But I do not have my way. Things have their way with me. It's as if I was being punished. Something's gotten into the nursery!...I don't know why. But then maybe, maybe I do and simply refuse to spill it. Still, I do not know why, just now. Now being forever, I do not know why. Everything escapes me including myself. Everything absconds except my autobiography. My autobiography is my anti-autobiography. My internal, infernal, fraternal eternal...

You'd think that being up here in the crushing blue, I'd have lots of time to reflect. Tell jokes. Think up funny stories. If only that were true. The only thing I think about is destruction. And I don't play with the idea. I actually carry it out. There are weapons in the soles of my shoes. My shoes are huge. They block out the sun, they are so huge. The heels, by themselves, are dark as the sub-basement of a skyscraper.

As I said, I don't play. I don't. I don't play. I have weapons in the soles of my shoes; a built-in electromagnetic-dualism from which lethal rays are released to strike down any target I desire. I am very accurate and I don't have to see my target to hit it. I merely think and it's leveled.

Today's target is the row of apartment buildings, I call them 'the castles', that face Central Park and line the street bearing its name. When I release my blasts, John Lennon's house is the first to go. Imagine it, if you will: beyond the tips of my Brogans, down on terra-firma, below me, I see the rumpled thighs of New

Jersey; and to the west, the erosion which is the shoulders of New York City. My pain has gotten out of hand. Imagine it: everywhere great fires rage. Floods and tornadoes legion. Ugly green spirals smash steel girders to paste. Buildings disintegrate. Columns, cupolas and finely detailed friezes commemorating self-hate and imperialism implode, fuse together forming tiny spheres weighing hundreds of trillions of tons. The surface of each sphere is amazingly smooth and reflective...

To describe it all would take a lifetime. So let me continue. It is beyond joy. Beyond festive. Trees vaporize. Thoughts atomize. To love is to vaporize. People are ripped from their Matisses and Häagen-Dazs and slip like spit down subway gratings as the city crumbles beneath my heels of radiation...

7

I apologize to the men and women; the doormen, handymen, receptionists, chambermaids, elevator operators, healthcare providers, cleaning ladies, janitors and other servants of empire forced to work in these feudal mousetraps. My heart is broken...and something else as well...because I too have worked in these buildings. As a pup, I helped my grandmother clean Mrs. Brown's toilet. Mrs. Brown of the white hands, the lost penny and the condescending hiss of the skirt. It was the beginning of my lethal apprenticeship. Soon, my grandmother had me cleaning the entire john. All summer, every monday and friday, I spun the Ajax round the porcelain...

Some years later, in these same buildings, I renovated the home of a famous Broadway actress. Her apartment was a veritable mansion. Every day I worked there, I never ate lunch in the same room. I had salami in the kitchen, pork in the living room, cream cheese in the rec room, peanut butter in the bath, moo goo gai pan in the necessary, beef jerky in the bedroom and wee- nies in the den. The crew boss was a Polish asshole named Frank. He had a moustache. He was a homosexual who believed money made the world go round. He was dizzy with the idea. The actress loved his moustache and he loved her ambition. I left the job before it was finished. My only concern was that I was finished. Life is the fumes escaping from a burning car...

8

Still, some things are sacred. Or, if not sacred then so fucking anti-autobiographical you don't dare mess with them. For example, the Port Authority Bus Terminal at 42nd St. and its inimitable denizens. The ones who sleep two to a box, the ones who light fires in their pockets, the ones who fight over the last red drop in the green glass bottle, the ones always with their hand out pretending to be pregnant begging for a quarter to help them catch that last bus back to Boca or Westchester and when they get it they're off and running to the bathroom to cop some wack to stick in their veins, the ones, the ones, the ones the police dogs lick up to. Yea, if there's a reason for a Zionist home- land, its doppleganger is the Port. Not to forget the Garden, that Eden of multicultural degradation, i.e. Penn Station, and the plethora of porno-palaces, t.g.i.f. twenty-four hour Kung Fu movie theaters, day-glo orange meat patties and Ma and Pa Iran- ian fixit, fuckit and munchie establishments, all which surround and glorify the P.A. like a doggie's necklace...

Yea, sure, some things must be cherished. Some things must be cherished and burnished like the tip of a gold syringe. Some things must be signed by unbearable experience. And I can hear it right now. People saying: "Why all this hostility? Why all this anger? Where did all this anger come from?" As if anger has a source like a faucet. And who says I'm angry? Maybe, maybe I'm just hungry...You should know better than that. You should know better than me. Anger, like the air we breathe, it doesn't need to be explained. At least not with faucets. So stop crying. Start complaining. Cause people'll say anything. Give you all kinds of arbitrary. Give you all kinds of arbitrary. Run you all kinds of advice: "You can wallow in your own shit", "You can dance in your own vomit", "You can drink your own piss, slice me a piece of that quiche, steep it in steroids, watch the sun rise over the Chernobyl in your peccadillos". All of it true. Wouldn't change a thing. But at the bottom of every crumb is the well of an idea, so: b-b-b-be it! Cause that's what I was doing when I plunged my bloody hand into that mound. That's exactly what I was doing when I found it was composed of used kitty litter, birdshot and an assortment of books describing the right way to a puppy's heart. Love a why. Love awry. Love away. Love lost. So I plunged, stayed, squatted, my hand immersed in some new degeneration, the birds swooping all around tweet-tweet unbroken chain, hypnotized, wre-wre-reconciled by their fluttering bodies and the cyclical music of their catatonic migration...

9

But beyond the mound, I saw a doorway, a doorway filled with white light. Through the white I could make out a field, a field overrun with tall dry grass and litter. At the far end of the field was a tumble-down fence. Beyond the fence was the Day St. Community Pool, alive with little black children splashing noisily and leaping into the boom-box air...

I stepped through that blinding doorway and found myself as you find me now: streaking across the sky against the horizon at anxious-making velocities. Everything: speed and indeterminacy. No duration. No grid of optimism. No radar to tell me what day it is, what to feel or what to dream. My course is jagged and fraught with violent changes of direction. Never ninety degrees to the poles but always in perfect resonance with some unknown yet unforgettable trajectory that tears the clothes from my body, the words from my mind and the leaves from the planet...

There is no beatitude. Only beatings. No lassitude. Just all out panic. No heavenly orchestra. Only the querulous ozone in endless stri-stri-stri-striangulation. No armaggedon. Simply a fart in the desert. For God is my copilot, I shall not want. He maketh me lie down in still waters. He restoreth my soul and I hate him for it...

Shh! I'm Talking to My Body Now

by Judy Bloomfield

I've watched you forever and no matter what I do,
you've betrayed me. Now I've got this feeling
that you never wanted to be here—spinning
in the air, existing among purple lilacs, forest pines. God's
  gifts
make your eyes water, force you to sneeze.

Fresh from the womb, your eyes shut hard
against the milk you couldn't digest,
and voices, the shimmering grey mother
curled over us. You couldn't bear it,
to look at this world. Was a past life more appealing?
Did you desire birth on a different a planet? Maybe you
wouldn't have needed so much prodding to live
in another solar system as a creature other than us.

Months later one eye opened, tried to focus
on blurry faces. The other needed two operations
before the pieces went together. Two
operations to raise the lid, get the light in
and create the scar, the dashed line
that even allows night vision.

I was six the first time you made me ask for death,
remember? So sick, I missed the first grade.

Through fevered lips I pushed out your hope to mother: *I
  wish I were dead.*
I think I felt the bed rock. You laughed at her tears,
chuckled during her pleas
to the doctor. You were the devil.
You made me sick, your allergies
keeping my immune system lost
among sinew, nerve endings, cells. How could you
keep a small girl from eating peanut butter
with her jelly? How could you keep her
from smearing mustard on hot dogs, or make her stay away
from cats, and dogs and horses?
How could I stop the bees from flying, from dipping
into flower after flower, spreading pollen through the air?

You dragged through puberty, reluctant, keeping breasts
flat, holding on to every egg so long I thought
there were none, and I read books on adoption.
Finally, one slipped down, the dark blood
proof of hope and future. I was safe,
lucky to cross over to men and their cocks,
a wrestling of first loves. My guard down,
this is how you got me. I knew not to get pregnant,
how to use birth control and I thought I was safe.
Sex was night shapes, soft skin, someone else's eyes, lazy
  mornings
turned poison by you. Camouflaged diseases crept on their
  knees
into nerve endings. Some invaded cells.

You wanted to be a seagull, suspended
over the ocean or an eel hugging the bottom of the sea.

I can't count the doctors. You and I in blue paper gowns
are always in synch, nodding and smiling at the nurses.
We are plotting escape.
No one wants to say cervical cancer.
I can't say it or tell it, but since the last surgery
you've been whispering it, planting it in my dreams.

I'm longing for the first grade, my tiny desk
the yellow smiley face pencils,
the Pink Pearl eraser, perfect and soft.
I want to erase my awkward cursive as if it were my life.
I want to start over.

Now the real battle begins. You and I,
squared off, fists raised. On my side:
vitamin A, Chinese herbs, meditation, and tarot.
Maybe God is behind me,
large hand gently shoving, because
after all this, I can't help but help you now.

The Bridge of Sighs

by Janet Kaplan

The 16th century Ponte dei Sospiri *connects the Ducal Palace
with the Venetian prisons. Its chamber is divided lengthwise by
partition so that persons going and those coming will not meet.*
— *Sturgis'* Illustrated Dictionary of Architecture and
Building, *1901*

Hanging vertically from the capstone
        above the thirty-odd-storied building
our country's flag seems just the flag

for a prison: its rust-red bars and the narrow
        night-blue window that contains
the stars. In the jurors' waiting room

I'm looking out past the rain over to Franklin Street
        where, on about the fifteenth floor,
a walkway covered by thick fish-tank glass

connects this courthouse to the prison.
        From time to time the glass-distorted
lawyers and prisoners appear, suspended

in watery limbo above Manhattan.
        Trapped in the jurors' room
dozens of us, judged unfit to serve

because we were victims of crime,
                    are returned here like repeat offenders
day after day for yet another judge to try us.

If by lunchtime I'm not picked
                    I'll visit Trinity Church again.
Yesterday an organist was playing a fugue,

pipes bellowing fire and brimstone.
                    Such a harsh resounding lesson
might have awoken the dead

but the men and smattering of women
                    asleep in the pews
held fast to their sleep.

One man pulled his soiled
                    woolen cap down over his face
and shifted closer to the wall.

I walked to the empty chancel, where I could turn
                    and look up at the player,
wondering if he knew his 'audience'

might be dying—or dead. He went on.
                    They seemed to go on too
despite the pipes' booms and heralds

as though each sleeper were beyond
                    ordinary range of earshot,
isolated gods

drifting in free fall though a silent
	universe, their sickly sleep
message enough

they wanted to live.
	I remembered, the night I was held
against the stairwell,

how I prayed my silence
	would keep me alive.
I remembered thinking, calmly,

that the silver gun protruding
	from his unzipped jacket
might have been a spike

like the ones that secured the criminal
	to his cross.
Maybe I pictured this because he

wore a cross around his neck,
	which he sucked on
as he told me what to do.

The bad dreams came later, the sweats,
	paranoia so fierce I couldn't look at a man
(even the one who lived with me)

without feeling my flesh tighten
	as though I were packed inside a cell.
If I could meet him again, if we could

redeem one another——but *its chamber divided*
        so that persons going and coming
will not meet——I'd tell him:

gods of division pace the bridge between our
        actions and who we've forgotten
we are. On and on

they play their irrelevant music
        while the boy you were burns
along with the rest of us.

Toxic   1984

by Kevin Young

CENTS in his
mouth like a scare-
crow stuffed

with news
print—a blanket
of words behind

him, infected,
undetected—hands
raised, braised

brown as turkey
legs. SMOKE
BOMB. SOUP

TO NUTS.
FIG 2 I —
EGG. Snake.

THAT EGG.
"BOY IT'S SURE
HOT HERE"—Bugs

Bunny, his goose
cooked over carrots—
GOLD. UNISON (INTRO)

All together now—
COMPOSED
TRUMPET SAX

(IMPROVED)—
his blue pork-
pie hat

a trumpet
muffler—
a squealer. MILES

DAVIS. GREGOR
MENDEL INVENTOR
OF X-RAY—

blowing down trom-
bones. Half
lives. Old school.

Head spun—
an electron,
popping

locking, anti-
matter. Eureka!
DR RADIUM

turning lead
paint to oil,
gold

standard. Agent
orange.
Noble gas,

periodic. Change
in his mouth
like a piggy bank

back, bills
unpaid
a beggar's dead

presidents
littering a hat—
VEHEMENT ALLEY CATS

GARBED A LA
KLU LUX KLAN PLAN
TO TORTURE THE—

notify next
of kin, a sign
on the doors

to spare
the first born.
Hands raised—

a saint
or a sinner, holy
rolling.

Snake eyes.
Dice kissed
for luck—

"PORKY'S PIG FEAT"
RACKATEER RABBIT—
C'mon bones

baby needs
new shoes.
Just wave your hands

in the air!
Arms raised
in praise

or a stick up—
nobody moves
nobody hurt.

Around his cop-
colored, hip
hop top

hat, the halo
a cameo—
INDUSTRY©.

LACK
OWDER
FROM AESOP'S

ER AND HIS CAT"—
blown up—
POOF—a hit

record, a vinyl
spill—
gone platinum.

INDUSTRY©.
I'm the King
of Rock

there is none higher—
a silent
canary down

a mine.
Drunk off
Molotov

cocktails—
moonshine. White
lighting. Acid

rain. 40 ounces
& a mule—
prescription,

placebo, he's out
to score
a fifth

of prevention,
a pound
of flesh. Antitode

anodyne—CENTS
in his mouth
like God's

unsaid name in a golem's—

28 September 1995

After Louie

by William Wilson

HERE'S HOW I THINK I GOT THE AIDS VIRUS.

It was the Friday night of Memorial Day weekend, 1980, and I'd gone out to the Spike, the premier New York leather bar of the era, over by the old West Side Highway, then still standing, in Chelsea. It was merely a first stop, a way into the night; eventually, I knew, I'd wind up several blocks from the Spike at the Mineshaft, a bracing if scary ten-minute walk through one of those big-city no-man's-lands, during which you hoped you wouldn't run into a gang of fag-baiting kids from the projects just east of there.

The Mineshaft was a leather sex club—though "sex" and "club" don't begin to do it justice—that European, Californian, and Australian leather queens made special trips to just to spend a few hours in, returning home with tales of its decadent, piss-drenched splendors. We New York leather queens agreed it was a special place, all right, but we'd been spoiled by having full-time access to it—and by New York's having been for a decade or so the center of the gay universe, more or less across the board. Studio 54; Diana Vreeland's Wildean aphorisms and Costume Institute dinners; drug dealers, already adept in the ways of the beeper, retailing a perplexing array of uppers and downers, coke and speed and acid from their rented limos; Andy and Truman and Halston (truly hideous role models, but calling the stylistic shots nevertheless); ever quickening art and fashion and music scenes; glamour and energy for as far as the eye could see.

The Mineshaft had its own glamour and certainly its energy. It anchored a corner in the meat-packing district, full of sides of beef hanging from hooks and paunchy men in bloody white coats, as nocturnal and eerie in its imagery as anything we leather queens could come up with, just south of 14th Street and a block from the river. There were two floors, one a basement and therefore perpetually dank, the other more like a demented frat house, complete with pool table and split-rail fence, perfect for sitting and posing, plus an open-air roof. You went in, you went upstairs, were checked out by the guys at the door (leather connoisseurs and past masters of raunch and sleaze), who made sure you weren't wearing khakis or Top-Siders or a Lacoste shirt. If you were, and if they nevertheless thought you had potential, you had the option of stowing the offending garments in the coatcheck, or going back down the stairs, your tail between your legs but, hey, no hard feelings, and coming back another night. (The worst thing to have on, however, was cologne, about which nothing much could be done, and out you went, feeling frustrated and sheepish.) Most people weren't, however, naked. Even the ones with enormous, selling-point dicks wouldn't have wanted to part with the leather jackets and chaps and vests that transformed them into icons of butchness, badness, and instant masculinity. In addition, there were usually a few uniforms around, California-highway-patrol numbers with spit-polished boots that laced up almost to the knees and those funny bulges on the outside of each leg just above them, plus visored helmets, reflective shades, badges, and nightsticks; or military ones, painstakingly authentic right down to the government-issue belt and cap and dog-tags and stripes, and, among true perfectionists, socks and underwear. True, such uniforms were most often pressed and pristine, qualities a lot of us weren't drawn to, but that was all right. At least somebody was really on the case, honing the old consciousness for fetishists everywhere.

Let me take some of your questions.

Were all the men "hot?" God, no. There were plenty of what we dismissed as trolls—one, with a replacement hip, ditto hand, a toupee, glass eye, I hope I'm getting this inventory right, was known as "Spare Parts"—but most were simply unappealing; still, they wanted to fondle you, if not blow you (or take you home for the night), just like anybody else. In addition, plenty were bland, meeting the terms of the door policy, but lacking imagination, working the room in hopes of an orgasm that had nothing to do with the visual. But there were usually enough that were hot, a dozen or more, say, to keep you on your toes, some true knockouts, some just paragons of high butch style. Who'd have guessed that, in fifteen years, half of them, so young and vigorous and muscular, preening and leering virtually nonstop, would be, you know what I'm about to say, don't you? dead or, as bad in a world where narcissism ruled, disfigured or cadaverous.

Were there any women at the Mineshaft? Very rarely. A handful of highly stylized, leatherclad, *Road Warrior* types who had earned the trust, and perhaps as important, the admiration of the guys and whom it was always a pleasure to see; I had always liked women more than men anyway, in every way but sexually. As far as I know, they didn't spend much time outside the barrooms (there were two, one upstairs, one down) and they were impeccably behaved, models of their own kind of ominous decorum.

Say something about the drugs. Of course it's impossible really to know, but I always assumed that practically everybody was on something. Coke was everywhere, with people making a pretense of being discreet about it, in a corner or in one of the johns or, if they had the necessary hand-to-nose coordination at three in the morning, just sitting in a shadow on the edge of the pool table; their maneuvers had to be repeated many times of course, as the previous noseful wore off. That was an inconvenience, but also represented a new chance to be bad, a rebel, not just a paper doll, and to show that you had some money to throw around (a come-on in the gay community of those days, though economics wasn't much of a motivator in this particular scene). People on speed or acid, and do ask me about MDA, had generally stoked up before coming out, since their stuff had an effect that went on for hours. Grass was everywhere. And poppers, and angel dust. Some locomotion was so impaired you could practically count the Quaaludes. And almost everybody had been drinking like crazy into the bargain.

So what's with this MDA? For a while it was my favorite drug. It wasn't expensive, one wet fingertipful (retail price, oh maybe $15) placed on the tongue could keep you going for hours. MDA made you think you were happy, it gave you an aspect of bona-fide friendliness (an advantage if you were constitutionally shy, as I was) and what passed for sensitivity, and it made you feel very, very sexy. That's why it had the nickname "lover's acid," although chemically I don't think it was related to acid at all, which in any event, the few times I ever tripped, was hard enough to handle on the couch in your own living room, let alone in a room at least some of whose occupants were wearing only motorcycle boots and a jock strap or dressed as Marine commandants. Later I would make the move to coke, which was in theory—all those tiny spoonfuls—more susceptible to fine-tuning.

How late did people stay at the Mineshaft? Often till dawn, or, on a Saturday night, straight through into the next day. I remember once getting home at 9:30 or so, that's AM, ragged and wet and bleary, and on my picturesque Village street a dapper old man, complete with white hair and mustache, had set up his easel and was already happily at work, on one of those crystalline New York spring mornings. It was one of the most shaming sights I'd ever seen.

What was so great about the roof? The air was revitalizing, you could actually watch the dawn, pink or misty, roll in, there weren't many people up there, and you could have sex—not that there wasn't anyplace in the Mineshaft where you couldn't have sex. You could do your coke in peace. I thought it was terribly romantic, actually, though most guys seemed to prefer the intense, maximally-populated, Boschian action downstairs.

What was the most shocking thing you ever saw at the Mineshaft? The most durable, ongoing shocker was the room with the tubs in it downstairs where people pissed on other people; the guys in the two or three perfectly conventional bathtubs would stay in them until they got so excited they had an orgasm, urine running down their chests or their chins. That could take hours. Other reporters might single out the slings, used for the then widespread practice of fisting. But that pales next to the one-shot shocker in which one man, late on a New Year's Eve, drove nails through the scrotum of another. He was very careful, perhaps even caring, and he obviously knew what he was doing. Someone later explained that all the nerves in the region are in the testicles themselves, not in the sac that houses them. But even if that's true, who came up with the idea in the first place?

Did everyone have a good time? By no means. Tempers flared, lovers fought with lovers, somebody once punched me in the stomach for no reason and promptly scurried away. People fell asleep on the benches that edged the upstairs bar, whether out of exhaustion or frustration it's hard to know. But most of us did seem to think we were having a good time. And, at the very least, it was an eyeful.

Whatever happened to the Mineshaft? It was closed in late 1985, along with a couple of bathhouses and a straight sex club or two. It was closed in a spirit that can only be described as hysterical, and only after great controversy between the office of the mayor (the hypocritical, distinctly not-out Ed Koch) and the gay community itself, as the AIDS epidemic gained momentum and no one had any idea where it was going. Really, what else could they do? We all knew it was the end of an era, its like never to be seen again. I remember thinking, the whole business—the epidemic, the falling away of all that decadence and energy and freedom, in gestation since the sixties—was the raw material of elegy.

So how do you think you got infected? No, not properly speaking *at* the Mineshaft. But let me tell you about Louie, whom I had run into there, or maybe walked with, south from the Spike, through the no-man's land.

I wasn't in love with Louie, whatever that might mean; I didn't even have a crush on him. But I liked his swagger—at its core buccaneerish more than bikerish—and his swarthiness. I don't mean he wore knee britches and an eyepatch (although both of us could have probably got right into the eyepatch; in fact, I subsequently bought one at the Pleasure Chest, the well-known sex-toys boutique). It's just that when you ran into him you didn't immediately think Harley-Davidson; for instance, although he wore leather like all the rest of us, he had only the shortest of beards and none of that out-of-control Hell's Angels hair and his forearms weren't a swirling mass of tattoos. He was maybe four years older than I was but he was worldlier and when we spent time together I half-felt he was taking care of me. He tended to have more drugs and it was his apartment, with its view of the entrance to the Lincoln Tunnel, that we went back to.

Louie was likable (if he deigned to notice you in the first place; he was also a snob) and obviously smart and apparently his own person. We were what you called "fuck-buddies," an indispensable phrase that meant you had sex only when you ran into each other at a bar and both of you were out alone; you didn't use the phone much (he did call once to invite me to a dinner party he was giving for some visiting German leather queens) and you didn't get jealous. You didn't "date." On the other hand, you did wonder what kept the two of you from forming a real attachment. I think Louie, less frozen in his ways than I was, might have been amenable to the idea.

It was, at any rate, an old-fashioned S&M relationship, with one of us "the top" and the other "the bottom" and a big wooden chest full of Louie's "toys" (handcuffs and restraints and tit clamps to put on the other person's nipples and butt plugs and on and on) and pretty much the full armamentarium of tried-and-true S&M techniques (hot wax, mild cat-o'-nine-tails action, binding and gagging; no shaving that I can recall). We switched off on the sexual roles, although Louie was a far more confident top than I was and I learned from him. Switching off was not unheard of in the world of male S&M but neither was it a common practice; most guys tended to be merely, rigidly top or bottom, and not particularly into altering their own behavior let alone breaking new people in. I would spend the night and we'd go to bed around daybreak under a big black fur pelt worthy of a Viking, on Louie's bed. Yes, we did cuddle; turns out you don't have to be in love—or to have just made gentle, respectful love—to cuddle. Then we'd go to a coffee shop, me still in my rancid gear, Louie slightly cleaned up, and have eggs and hash browns. Typically, Louie would be on his way to Stompers, the impeccably stocked boot shop he owned on Fourth Street, just west of Sheridan Square.

What I haven't made explicit, though it must seem obvious, is how, at the end of one of these sessions, the top fucked the bottom, a final humiliation during which he compared the bottom to a cock-needy woman. Or the like. Or made the bottom beg for it. And made the bottom suck his dick clean when he was finished. This wasn't just Louie; it was standard S&M operating procedure. And then everybody got to go to bed.

I had always hated getting fucked. It really hurt unless your anus was stretched out, which it wasn't likely to be unless you'd been happily in that position many times before. I'd been fucked perhaps a dozen times since the summer of 1968, when I arrived in New York to serve as the Yale College representative on the Saks Fifth Avenue Men's College Fashion Board, meant to convince freshmen-to-be—alongside the Princeton and Harvard and Columbia, etc., representatives—that they needed a blazer and a couple of suits and a tweed jacket and maybe a tuxedo and if you were really doing your job (not that any of us were) a whole lot more, in advance of arrival on campus. To a degree they really did need them. In 1968 there were still dining-hall dress codes at Yale (not to mention parietal rules and distributional requirements and a strictly numerical grading system). By the next year, though, it was all over and nobody was putting on a rep tie and a herringbone jacket with scrambled-egg stains on the sleeves to go to dinner, let alone breakfast; moreover, many people's weekend dates were being billeted in their suites, and academic matters had become much easier to finesse with the advent of a honors/pass/fail policy. Like the shuttering of the Mineshaft, it represented the end of an era. Even Yale had made it, belatedly, in 1968, into the sixties.

1968 was also the summer I came out, at least to myself. I was sharing a sublet with five classmates, quite an upscale one actually, complete with grand piano and access to an interior garden, on far west Bleecker Street. I found out I was gay one night on my way home from Saks, wearing a chalk-stripe suit and Guccis as I was walking along Christopher Street, already a major cruising street all the way to Sixth Avenue, though my radar hadn't yet picked up on it, and I was just trying to get home. I had, however, a couple of minutes earlier picked up on a dirty-blond juvenile delinquent, a real Stanley Kowalski type, tight jeans and T-shirt, motorcycle boots, a pack of Marlboros rolled into his sleeve. Our meeting was the collision of two distinct iconographies, it was very exciting to me for that reason, and the next thing I knew we were making out in the entryway of one of those insanely picturesque little townhouses on, it's true, Gay Street. We didn't do more than kiss and touch, but I had an instantaneous orgasm in my blue, oxford-cloth boxer shorts. It was the first indication of a big problem—premature ejaculation—that would plague me till I discovered cocaine. Mostly, though, it allowed me to understand why dating at college had been, for me, such a pantomime of reluctance and awkwardness. As for my first paragon of masculinity, his name turned out to be Shelly and many years later I would see him on the F train, working intently on a lap-rug-sized needlepoint of Marilyn Monroe with her pleated skirt being lifted up by the steam from a subway grating. You know the shot.

But about anal sex. You know, you come out, you work to learn the customs of the country, you make an effort to fit in, you may well be cute but you surely aren't confident, you try to be obliging to the new people you're meeting, most of whom, as it happens, want to fuck you, or at least think they want to fuck you, up the ass. Or, in Yeats's timeless formulation, "Love has pitched its mansion in the place of excrement." I didn't like it then and I've never liked it, plus I didn't want to fuck somebody else up the ass either, a major shortfall of both bonhomie and hospitality, but I didn't have anything better to suggest, let alone enough technique to move somebody else in that direction. I think I knew what *I* really wanted to do (namely, execute a painstaking impersonation of my partner, wearing his pitted out T-shirt and lighting up one of his Marlboros, but I couldn't imagine that transformation ranked high on most other people's sexual menus).

So Louie would fuck me or I would fuck Louie, depending on the night's balance of power. As I've already said about a hundred times, I didn't like it (Louie seemed to like it fine, and moaned and writhed, although that could of course have been a version of what wives are so famously said to do). I did see the logic of it, a fitting culmination to the politics and pain of sex.

How do I know that it was Louie who infected me? I don't of course. Conjecture. It was the last time, that Memorial Day weekend of 1980, I would ever be fucked; in the previous half-decade I'd been fucked, as best I can reconstruct, no more than three or four times. I developed full-blown, as they say, AIDS twelve years later, pretty much par for the course for a "longterm survivor." Louie was looking sick by 1986 (I no longer "played" with him; he'd found a lover by then, who would die some time after Louie did, in 1989). Of course, in 1980, and for the next few years, nobody knew how AIDS was transmitted, let alone what the disease's timetable was. Moreover, that timetable was enormously perplexing; a very few people had been getting sick and dying—the diagnosis was typically hepatitis—even in the late seventies. Other obviously life-in-the-fast-lane types were fine for a long time, only eventually crumbling. Some didn't crumble, and haven't since. In the early eighties there still wasn't a test (and no possible treatments anyway), and for a couple of years thereafter nobody understood what, exactly, testing positive really meant.

Anyway, Louie was dead. I didn't go to the memorial service, but I had gone to a kind of premature memorial concert the year before, while he was fragile but still alive; it was music about the epidemic, though you can't prove it by me, who can hardly tell a polka from a concerto. Anyway, it turned out that Louie didn't just run a boot shop; he was also a composer and a composer who'd studied with Elliott Carter and been nominated for a Pulitzer. Which brings us to the part of the Louie story I like best.

I had first met Louie in Rome in the summer of 1969, in the Piazza Navona, a calculatedly theatrical square that served, appropriately, as a gay cruising ground in a city famously hostile to bars. I was sitting on the rim of that beyond-baroque fountain by Bernini, the middle one showing the four rivers, one for each corner of the earth—the Danube, the Nile, the Ganges, the New World's de la Plata. I loved it less because it was so over-the-top exuberant than because it was all about geography, a favorite pastime of mine; for the record, I can still name the 192 independent nations of the world in alphabetical order.

Louie was one of those people who'd weighed 350 pounds, loathed himself, and perhaps in an attempt to erect a barrier between himself and the world, had gone into the priesthood, rich in its own full-cut outfits and fleshly obsessions, of course.

Then he'd somehow lost all the weight, discovering in the process that people—especially men—reacted to him, wanted in on that swarthiness and swagger. Now he'd gotten himself a Prix de Rome and was settled in for a couple of years at the American Academy. We talked for an hour or so. That was that. But I never forgot him, a bit like the old guy in *Citizen Kane* who as a youth sees the girl in a white dress on the ferry to New Jersey, doesn't so much as speak to her, yet can never forget her.

The first time I saw Louie in New York I immediately remembered him, but for a year or so I kept it to myself. It was too risky: you give somebody an advantage, an upper hand when you admit to remembering him, and he, I could tell, didn't remember me. Finally I told him, en route from the Spike to the Mineshaft one night. He wasn't put off, as I might have been, and may have been flattered. There wasn't a big reaction. But it was for me one of those super-charged, life-is-really-something moments. Even if you ignored the fated-to-meet-and-meet-again interpretation, it still said something about the smallness, some would say claustrophobia, of the gay world, the preciseness and summonability of human memory, a sexual brotherhood that went on and on. At least until somebody, or everybody, died.

Ugly

by Star Black

Sometimes, within the walls' white profusions
nothing appears sadder than a wasp dying upon
a screen, unable to distinguish between wire
and liberty, bashing, searching for release

from what seems an airy opening, what seems
volition among empowering trees, stalking on
prickly wasp feet up and down the imprisoning
plane, but to observe this, in pain, is to be far

from larger requiems, trigger-struck refrains.
Still, when the air is sullen and within beams,
the thug bug seems defenseless, denuded of all

its sting, and must be set free, gingerly, to be
renewed for its elemental entombing. It is black
and lives outside, unaware of what's symbolized.

Upcoming Issues

FUTURE ISSUES: *Every Picture Tells a Story,* on the static image as a point of departure/catalyst. Including but not limited to family snapshots, billboards, children's faces on milk cartons, subway advertisements, etc. Especially interested in stories/poems that respond to art/photography.

Imminent Danger, on the situations that test the limits of our psyches and hearts, taking calculated and uncalculated risks, physical danger versus psychological danger; paranoia, thrill-seeking, getting lost; peril and risk in love and sex; danger to our health and our environments; devils, war, natural disasters, vulnerability, protection.

Global City Backlist

All *Global City Press* publications are available at your local bookstore (in stock or by special order) or through our distributor, Consortium Book Sales & Distribution (1-800-283-3572).

Contributors

STAR BLACK is the author of *Double Time*, a book of poems released by The Groundwater Press, and an associate editor of *Pacnassus: Poetry in Review*. She works in New York City as a photographer.

JUDY BLOOMFIELD is a poet, living, working and creating in Manhattan.

DENISE DUHAMEL is the author of four full-length books of poetry, *Kinky, Girl Soldier, The Woman with Two Vaginas* and *Smile!* and a chapbook *How the Sky Fell* (Pearl Editions, 1996.) Her poems appear in previous issues of *Global City Review, Ontario Review, Third Coast,* and *Partisan Review.*

CHESTER KEETON FREEMAN is originally from southern Louisiana. He has studied writing at LSU and in the Graduate Writing Program at New York University. He works as a freelance editor. "Dogwood " is part of a novel-in-progress: *The World According to My Tongue.*

CULLEN GERST is from Berkeley, California. This story is for W.G., and also G.G.

JANET KAPLAN earned her MFA degree in poetry at Sarah lawrence College. Her poems have appeared in numerous publications including *Ms., The Sow's Ear,* and *Yearbook of American Poetry.* Her manuscript, *The Groundnote,* was a finalist for the 1996 Beatrice Hawley Award from Alice James Books. In 1984 she initiated the Trained Poets project (poetry posters for subways and buses). She currently lives in Brooklyn and teaches creative writing at the State University of New York, College at Old Westbury.

HELEN KIM is both a poet and a fiction writer. Her most recent poem, "Father," will appear in *Goldfinch* this May. Her first novel, *The Long Season of Rain,* will be published by Henry Holt and Company in the fall of 1996. She is a recipient of a grant from the New Jersey State Council on the Arts as well as a residency at The Macdowell Colony. She teaches literature and creative writing at Montclair State University.

JUDY KRAVIS teaches French literature and tends an Irish garden. She is the author of *Tea With Marcel Proust,* editor of *Teaching Literature: Writers and Teachers Talking,* and is working on a book of interviews with fish out of water in Ireland: *Irish Independents.*

PAUL LISICKY has published fiction in a variety of publications including *Mississippi Review*, *Provincetown Arts*, *Carolina Quarterly*, and in the anthologies *Men on Men 6* and *Flash Fiction*. A recipient of NEA and Michener Fellowships, he recently completed a novel titled *Lawnboy*. He lives in Provincetown, Massachusetts.

MICHAEL LUNNEY writes plays and stories. An adaptation of "The History of Misogyny" was produced at Synchronicity Space (along with other short plays) and performed by his father, Leo Lunney.

CHRISTINE LIOTTA is a writer and freelance editor. She has been published in numerous arts and literary magazines, including *Glimmer Train*, *Hanging Loose*, *Tema Celeste*, *Mudfish*, and the *National Poetry Magazine of the Lower East Side*. She lives in Long Island City, New York, and is at work on a book of short fiction, *Car Trouble*.

RACHEL MIKOS-NAFT is an artist, writer and translator who lives in New York City. She is currently working on a book of translations of the stories of Frigyes Karinthy for Corvina Press in Budapest.

WILLIAM POPE.L is a three-headed black who is falling into the sun. He is a performance artist and teaches at Bates College in Lewiston, Maine.

VIRGINIA BETH SHIELDS grew up in a small working-class poor rural farming community in the Appalachian foothills of South Carolina. Two fine arts degrees and numerous solo and group exhibitions later she is creating visual art which examines her own family history as a method for exploring personal identity. "Name" is part of a larger photo-text based crossmedia work she is currently working on entitled "Seed".

WILLIAM WILSON, who still lives in New York, is working on a memoir.

KEVIN YOUNG's first book *Most Way Home* was a National Poetry Series winner published by Wm. Morrow/Quill. An assistant professor in English & African American Studies at University of Georgia, he has held a Stegner Fellowship in Poetry and several MacDowell Colony residencies. Currently he is completing a manuscript on the late artist Jean-Michel Basquiat, from which "Toxic" is taken. Several of Young's poems are featured alongside Basquiat's works on paper in the exhibition *Two Cents*, on view at Otis College Gallery, Los Angeles, from September-October 1996.